11-02

easy Afghans

50 Knit and Crochet Projects

Family Circle

easy
Afghans
50 Knit and Crochet Projects

Sixth&Spring Books
New York

Sixth&Spring Books
233 Spring Street
New York, NY 10013

Editor-in-Chief
Trisha Malcolm

Book Editor
Michelle Lo

Art Director
Chi Ling Moy

Manager, Book Division
Theresa McKeon

Designer
Shirley Levi

Managing Editor
Jean Guirguis

Copy Editor
Annemarie McNamara

Editorial Assistant
Anna Bolton

Contributors
Betty Christiensen

Yarn Editor
Veronica Manno

Technical Editors
Carla Scott
Karen Greenwald

Production Manager
David Joinnides

President and Publisher, Sixth&Spring
Art Joinnides

Family Circle Magazine
Editor-in-Chief
Susan Kelliher Ungaro

Executive Editor
Barbara Winkler

Creative Director
Diane Lamphron

Library of Congress Catalog-in-Publication Data
Easy Afghans: 50 knit and crochet projects/ [Editor in chief, Trisha Malcolm].
    p.cm.
At head of title: Family circle easy knitting.
ISBN 1-931543-01-1
    1. Afghans (Coverlets) 2. Knitting--Patterns. 3. Crocheting--Patterns. I. Title: Family
circle easy knitting easy afghans. II. Malcolm, Trisha, 1960- III. Family circle easy knitting

TT825.E2794 2001
746.43'40437--dc21

                                                                              2001020548

Table of Contents

Easy-on-You

Oh-so-simple…whip up cozy, comfortable weekend warmers in a flash!

Afghan Express

for beginner knitters

Combining two strands of chenille yarn accentuates the incredibly soft hand of this textured beach-friendly basketweave afghan designed by Gitta Schrade. The "Afghan Express" first appeared in the Spring/Summer '99 issue of *Family Circle Easy Knitting*.

MATERIALS

■ *Thick & Quick Chenille* by Lion Brand Yarn Co., 5oz/142g skeins, each approx 101yd/94m (acrylic/rayon)
20 skeins in #098 off-white
■ Size 17 (12.75mm) circular needle, 31½"/80cm long OR SIZE TO OBTAIN GAUGE

FINISHED MEASUREMENTS

■ 82" x 119"/208cm x 302cm

GAUGE

5 sts and 8 rows over pat st using size 17 (12.75mm) needle.
TAKE TIME TO CHECK YOUR GAUGE.

Note

Work with 2 strands of yarn held tog throughout.

PATTERN STITCH

Row 1 (RS) *K4, p4; rep from * to end.
Rows 2-4 K the knit sts and p the purl sts.
Row 5 *P4, k4; rep from * to end.
Rows 6-8 K the knit sts and p the purl sts.
Rep rows 1-8 for pat st.

THROW

With 2 strands of yarn held tog, cast on 4 sts. Work in St st for 4 rows, casting on 4 sts at end of last row—8 sts.
Next row (RS) K4, p4; cast on 4 sts—12 sts.
Next row P4, k4, p4.

Next row K4, p4, k4.
Next row P4, k4, p4, cast on 4 sts—16 sts.
Next row [K4, p4] twice; cast on 4 sts—20 sts.
Next row [P4, k4] twice, p4.
Next row [K4, p4] twice, k4. Work in pat, inc 4 sts at end of next 2 rows. Cont in this way to cast on 4 sts each side every 3rd and 4th row (working inc sts into pat st) until there are 164 sts on needle. Work even in pat for 4 rows more. Bind off 4 sts at beg of next 2 rows. Work 2 rows even. Rep last 4 rows until 4 sts rem. Work in St st for 4 rows. Bind off.

Southwest Stunner

for intermediate knitters

This spicy throw, knit in a linen stitch, was inspired by many sources—Navajo blankets, desert dawns, and Southwestern sunsets. Customize this textural and rustic design by changing the colors of the stripes to coordinate with your existing décor. The "Southwest Stunner" first appeared in the Fall '95 issue of *Family Circle Easy Knitting*.

MATERIALS

- *1824* by Mission Falls 1¾oz/50g, each approx 85yd/78m (wool)
  9 balls in #011 poppy (A)
  5 balls #009 nectar (B)
  4 balls #010 russet (C), #021 denim (D), #016 thyme (E)
  3 balls #013 gold (F)
- Size 9 (5.5mm) circular needle, 36"/90cm long OR SIZE TO OBTAIN GAUGE

FINISHED MEASUREMENTS

- 35" x 56½"/89cm x 143.5cm

GAUGE

24 sts and 40 rows to 4"/10cm on size 9 (5.5mm) needles in linen st.
TAKE TIME TO CHECK YOUR GAUGE.

Notes

1 Afghan is worked back and forth on a circular needle to accommodate all sts.
2 All sts in pat are slipped purlwise.

LINEN ST

(Over an even number of sts)
Row 1 (RS) Wyib, sl1, k1, *wyif, sl1, wyib, k1; rep from * to end.
Row 2 Wyif, sl1, p1, *wyib, sl1, wyif, p1; rep from * to end.
Rep rows 1 and 2 for linen st.

AFGHAN

With circular needle and A, cast on 210 sts. Work in linen st and stripe pat as foll: *[8 rows A, 2 rows C, 2 rows A, 6 rows C, 2 rows A, 2 rows C, 10 rows A, 2 rows B, 2 rows A, 14 rows B], 6 rows D, 4 rows F, 14 rows E, 4 rows F, 6 rows D, 2 rows A; rep from * 5 times more, then work bet [ ]'s once. Bind off all sts.

FINISHING

Weave in ends.

The Natural Touch
for beginner knitters

This rough-hewn garter stitch and rib patterned afghan lends itself to endless afternoons and evenings spent curled up with a favorite book or knitting project. First featured in the Fall '97 issue of *Family Circle Easy Knitting*, the afghan's cuddly feel and classic shade will make it an indispensable addition to a family room or den for years to come.

MATERIALS
- *Al•Pa•Ka* by Lion Brand Yarn Co., 1¾oz/50g skeins each approx 107yd/98m (acrylic/alpaca/wool)
  19 skeins in #124 camel
- Size 13 (9mm) circular needle 40"/100cm long OR SIZE TO OBTAIN GAUGE

FINISHED MEASUREMENTS
- 40" x 56"/101.5cm x 142cm

GAUGE
12 sts and 18 rows to 4"/10cm over k2, p2 rib (blocked) and over garter rib pat (blocked) with 2 strands held tog.
TAKE TIME TO CHECK GAUGE.

Note
2 strands are held together throughout.

STITCHES USED
K2, p2 rib
(Even number of sts)
Row 1 (RS) *K2, p2; rep from * to end.
Row 2 K the knit sts and p the purl sts. Rep row 2 for the k2, p2 rib pat.
Garter rib pattern
Rows 1 and 2 Knit
Rows 3 and 4 Purl
Rep these 4 rows for garter rib pat.

THROW
With 2 strands held tog throughout, cast on 120 sts.

Pat sequence #1
*Work 24 sts in k2, p2 rib, 24 sts in garter rib pat; rep from * once, end 24 sts in k2, p2 rib. Cont in pats as established for 36 rows.

Beg pat sequence #2
*Work 24 sts in garter rib pat, 24 sts in k2, p2 rib; rep from * once, end 24 sts in garter rib pat. Cont in pats as established for 36 rows. Rep pat sequence #1 and #2 three times more, end with pat sequence #1. Bind off. Block throw to measurements.

Cable Comforts

for beginner knitters

Rich yarns and an added twist on traditional cables give this afghan a luscious loftiness that will delight the senses in any season. A simple garter-stitch edging and long, indulgent fringe add an extra touch of luxury. Designed by the Berroco Design Studio, the "Cable Comforts" afghan first appeared in the Spring/Summer '98 issue of *Family Circle Easy Knitting*.

MATERIALS

- *Illusions* by Classic Elite Yarns, 1¾oz/50g hanks, each approx 110yd/100m (cotton/rayon/poly)
  15 skeins in #1716 natural (A)
- *La Gran Mohair* 1½oz/40g balls, each approx 90yd/81m (mohair/wool/nylon)
  18 skeins in #6516 natural (B)
- Size 10 (6mm) circular needle, 29"/74cm long OR SIZE TO OBTAIN GAUGE
- Size H/8 (5mm) crochet hook
- Cable needle (cn)

FINISHED MEASUREMENTS

- 42" x 51"/105.5cm x 129cm excluding fringe

GAUGE

16 sts and 20 rows to 4"/10cm over cable pat using size 10 (6mm) needles and 1 strand A and B held tog.
TAKE TIME TO CHECK YOUR GAUGE.

Note

Use 2 strands held together throughout.

AFGHAN

With one strand A and B held tog, cast on 169 sts on circular needle. Working back and forth in rows, work cable pat as foll:
Row 1 (RS) K11, *p3, k6; rep from *, end p3, k11.
Row 2 and all even rows K5, p6, *k3, p6; rep from * end k5.
Row 3 K11, *p3, sl next 3 sts to cn and hold to back, k3, k3 from cn (6-st RC), p3, k6; rep from * end p3, 6-st RC, k5.
Row 5 K5, 6-st RC, *p3, k6, p3, 6-st RC; rep from * end p3, k11.
Rows 7, 9 and 15 Rep row 1. **Row 11** Rep row 5.
Row 13 Rep row 3. **Row 16** Rep row 2. Rep rows 1-16 for cable pat a total of 16 times or 256 rows. Piece measures approx 51"/129cm from beg. Bind off in pat.

FRINGE

Cut two 12"/30.5 strands of A for one fringe. With crochet hook, pull through first st on cast-on edge. Cut 2 strands of B and pull through next st. Alternate A and B across cast-on edge then bound-off edge sts. Steam afghan lightly. Trim fringe evenly.

Gingham Glory

for beginner knitters

Alternating and combining two different-colored yarns produces an intriguing gingham look. Knit one square in white, one in lavender, and a third by holding the two together for a heathered effect. When arranged, the squares produce a fresh plaid pattern perfect for a child's room or the sunniest nook in the house. The "Gingham Glory" afghan first appeared in the Fall '98 issue of *Family Circle Easy Knitting*.

MATERIALS

◾ *Jiffy* by Lion Brand Yarn Co., 3oz/85g balls, each approx 135yd/121.5m (acrylic)
  7 balls in #100 white (A)
  9 balls in #144 blue (B)
◾ Size 15 (10mm) circular needle, 29"/74cm OR SIZE TO OBTAIN GAUGE

FINISHED MEASUREMENTS

◾ 40" x 56"/101.5cm x 142cm

GAUGE

8 sts and 13 rows to 4"/10cm over St st with 2 strands held tog, using size 15 (10mm) needles.
TAKE TIME TO CHECK YOUR GAUGE.

Note

1 Two strands of yarn are held tog throughout.
2 When changing colors, twist yarns tog on WS to prevent holes.

THROW

COLOR SEQUENCE 1

Cast on 18 sts A and B, 18 sts with 2 strands A, 18 sts A and B, 18 sts with 2 strands A, 18 sts A and B. Work in St st for 8"/20.5cm, end with a WS row.

COLOR SEQUENCE 2

K 18 sts with 2 strands B, 18 sts A and B, 18 sts with 2 strands B, 18 sts A and B, 18 sts with 2 strands B. Work for 8"/20.5cm, end with a WS row.
Rep color sequence 1 and 2 twice more, then color sequence 1 once more. Bind off.

FINISHING

Cut 11"/28cm lengths of B for fringe. Holding 2 strands tog, fringe all sides.

Spring Foliage
for beginner knitters

The first leaves of spring burst open on Gitta Schrade's cool cotton throw featuring the freshest colors of the season and just a touch of texture. The intarsia leaves are knit in individual squares, joined together, and finished with a striped garter- and stockinette-stitch border. Embroidered details on the leaves add surface interest and a realistic touch. This spring delight first appeared in the Spring/Summer '00 issue of *Family Circle Easy Knitting*.

MATERIALS
- *Sugar 'n Cream* 4ply by Lily®, 1 lb cone each approx 85yd/74m (or 2.5oz/70.9g each approx 120 yd/109m) (cotton)
  2 cones plus 2 balls in #04 ecru (MC)
  3 balls each in #70 lime (A), #16 dk pine (B), #48 mauve (E), #09 navy (F), #42 rose (G), #88 mocha (H)
  2 balls each in #55 lt green (C), #62 emerald (D)
- One pair size 7 (4.5mm) needles OR SIZE TO OBTAIN GAUGE.
- Size E/4 (3.5mm) crochet hook
- Embroidery needle
- Two 14"/35.5cm square pillow forms

FINISHED MEASUREMENTS
Afghan
- 75½" x 49½"/192cm x 126cm

Pillow
- 14" x 14"/35.5cm x 35.5cm

GAUGE
19 sts and 26 rows to 4"/10cm over St st using size 7 (4.5mm).
TAKE TIME TO CHECK YOUR GAUGE.

AFGHAN
Make 15 Squares as foll:
Chart 1 (Make 3)
With MC, cast on 62 sts. Work chart rows 1 to 84, working leaf motif as foll: 1 square each A, B and D.
Chart 2 (Make 3)
With MC, cast on 62 sts. Work chart rows 1 to 84, working leaf motif as foll: 1 square each A, B, and C.
Chart 3 (Make 3)
With MC, cast on 62 sts. Work chart rows 1 to 84, working leaf motif as foll: 1 square each A, B, and D.

Chart 4 (Make 3)
With MC, cast on 62 sts. Work chart rows 1 to 84, working leaf motif as foll: 1 square each B, C, and D.
Chart 5 (Make 3)
With MC, cast on 62 sts. Work chart rows 1 to 84, working leaf motif as foll: 1 square each A, C, and D.

FINISHING
Block squares to measurements.
With contrast color of choice embroider veins, using photo as guide.
Sew squares tog as desired.

EDGING
Stitch pattern
*6 rows garter st, 4 rows St st, 10 rows garter st, 2 rows St st; rep from * for st pat.
With E, cast on 25 sts. Work in st pat, changing colors when going from garter st to St st as desired. Work until band fits along one side of afghan plus 5½"/13cm (for corner). Cont in this way until all 4 pieces are worked. Sew bands in place.

With RS facing, crochet hook and A, work 1 rnd sl st around entire afghan, 1 stitch in from edge, then work 1 rnd sc around entire afghan, using sl st rnd as base.

PILLOWS
MAPLE PILLOW
Front
Make 1 square Chart A, using col A for leaf.
Back
With E, cast on 60 sts. Work in St st using colors for edging.

FINISHING
Block pieces. Embroider veins. With WS tog, sew 3 seams. Insert pillow form, sew closed.

CHESTNUT PILLOW
Front
Make 1 square Chart C, using col B for leaf.
Back
Work as for Maple Pillow, beg with any col but E for different look.

FINISHING
As for Maple Pillow.

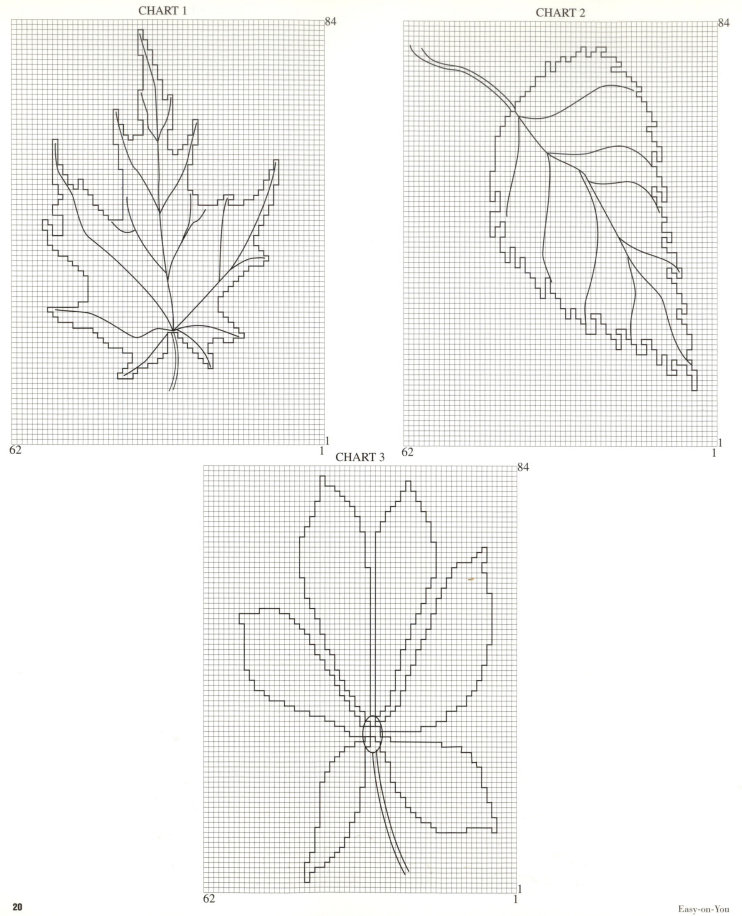

CHART 1

84

62

1

1

CHART 2

84

62

1

1

CHART 3

84

62

1

CHART 4
84

CHART 5
84

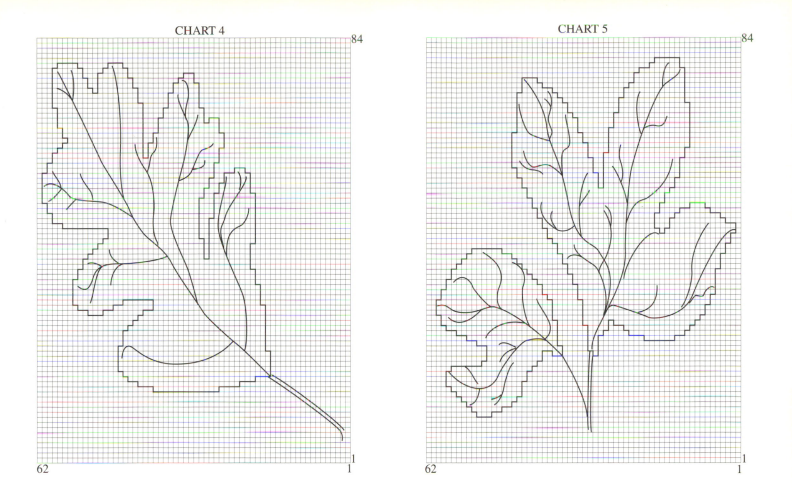

Whip-stitched Wonder

for beginner knitters

A perfect project for novice knitters or those on the go, Barbara Fimbel's casual and simple stockinette-stitch afghan is knit in individual squares. The blocks are arranged, alternating knit and purl sides, then whip-stitched together with contrasting yarn. The edges are finished with the same whip-stitched touch. This "Whip-stitched Wonder" first appeared in the Winter '00/'01 issue of *Family Circle Easy Knitting*.

MATERIALS

- *Turnberry Tweed* by Reynolds/JCA, 3½oz/100g balls, each approx 220yd/198m (wool)
  4 balls each in #87 green, #67 lt green, #55 lt blue, #36 blue devon
- *Devon* by Reynolds/JCA, 1¾oz/50g balls, each approx 82yd/74m (wool)
  4 balls in #20 black
- One pair size 13 (9mm) needles OR SIZE TO OBTAIN GAUGE
- Tapestry needle

FINISHED MEASUREMENTS

- 48" x 60"/122cm x 152cm

GAUGE

10 sts and 13 rows to 4"/10cm over St st using size 13 (9mm) needles.
TAKE TIME TO CHECK YOUR GAUGE.

Note

Hold 2 strands of yarn together throughout.

AFGHAN

Square

Cast on 10 sts. Work in St st for 4"/10cm. Bind off.
Make 45 squares in each color.

FINISHING

Block squares. Using 2 strands of black held tog, whip stitch squares tog in a random manner. Place some squares with St st facing and some with rev St st facing. Sew squares in strips of 12 squares by 15 squares. Block afghan.

Angular Accents

for intermediate knitters

Barbara Fimbel's two-toned graphic motif throw is pieced together with interlocking mitered-corner squares, creating the optical illusion of a complicated pattern. In reality, the garter-stitched squares are simple to knit and artfully arranged. The "Angular Accents" afghan first appeared in the Winter '00/'01 issue of *Family Circle Easy Knitting*.

MATERIALS

- *Soft* by Red Heart®, 5oz/225g skeins, each approx 328yd/302m (acrylic)
  6 skeins each in #7821 medium blue (A) and 7615 lt celery (B)
- One pair size 8 (5mm) needles OR SIZE TO OBTAIN GAUGE
- Tapestry needle

FINISHED MEASUREMENTS

- 44" x 60"/111.5cm x 152cm

GAUGE

20 sts and 40 rows to 4"/10cm over garter using size 8 (5mm) needles
TAKE TIME TO CHECK YOUR GAUGE.

STRIPED SQUARE

(Make 75)
With color B, cast on 43 sts.
Row 1 Knit. Row 2 Attach color A, k 20, k3tog, k 20. Row 3 Knit
Row 4 With color B, k19, k3tog, k19.
Row 5 Knit Rep rows 2-5 until 3 sts rem. Next row Sl 1, k2 tog, psso.

PLAIN SQUARE

(Make 36)
With color A, work as for striped squares without changing colors.

FINISHING

First row, sew 4 striped squares tog with the top of each square facing the tops of the other squares, taking care to match stripes. Rep twice more. Holding large squares as diamonds, sew into a row alternating with solid squares also held as diamonds (see photo).
Last 7 rows, sew 3 squares tog as before, leaving off the top square. With the tops facing, sew under the first row as shown, then sew in place again, alternating with plain squares. Work in ends.

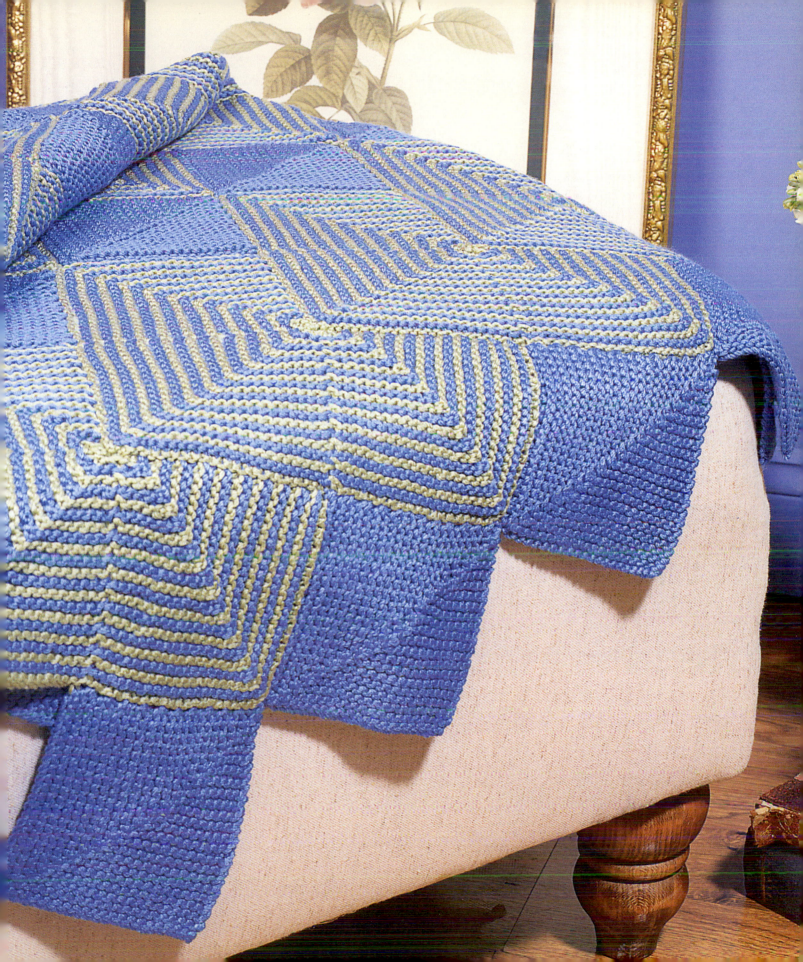

Medallion Medley

for beginner knitters

This clever collection of crocheted hexagons is created in individual medallions, which are then whip-stitched together. Crocheted in a variegated yarn of sea-inspired blues and greens, the effect is dazzling and surprisingly simple to make. Designed by Maria Matteucci, the "Medallion Medley" was first featured in the Winter '00/'01 issue of *Family Circle Easy Knitting*.

MATERIALS

- *Décor* by Patons®, 3½oz/100g balls, each approx 210yd/192m (acrylic/wool)
  9 balls in #1692 blue multi
- Size G/6 (4.5mm) crochet hook OR SIZE TO OBTAIN GAUGE

FINISHED MEASUREMENTS

- 42" x 56"/106.5cm x 142cm

GAUGE

Each medallion approx 7"/17.5cm wide using size G/6 (4.5mm) crochet hook. TAKE TIME TO CHECK YOUR GAUGE.

AFGHAN

(Make 48 medallions)
Ch 3, join with a sl st to first ch to form ring.
Rnd 1 Ch 3 (counts as 1 dc), work 11 dc in ring. Join with sl st on top of the 3rd ch.
Rnd 2 Ch 3 (counts as 1 dc), 2 dc in same sp, ch 3, [skip 1 dc, 3 dc in next dc, ch 3], 5 times, join with sl st on top of 3rd ch.

Rnd 3 Ch 3, 1 dc in same sp, 1 dc in next dc, 2 dc in next dc, [ch 3, skip ch 3, 2 dc in next dc , dc in next dc] 5 times, ch 3, join with sl st on top of 3rd ch.
Rnd 4 Ch 3, 1 dc in same sp, dc in next 3 dc, 2 dc in next dc, [ch 3, skip ch 3, 2 dc in next dc, dc in next dc, 2 dc in next dc] 5 times, ch 3, join with sl st on top of 3rd ch.
Rnd 5 Ch 3, 1 dc in same sp, dc in next 5 dc, 2 dc in next dc, skip ch 3, ch 3, [2 dc in next dc, dc in next 5 dc, 2 dc in next dc] 5 times, ch 3, join with sl st on top of 3rd ch.
Rnd 6 Ch 3, 1 dc in same sp, dc in next 7 dc, 2 dc in next dc, skip ch 3, ch 3, [2 dc in next dc, dc in next 7 dc, 2 dc in next dc] 5 times, join with sl st on top of the 3rd ch. Fasten off.

FINISHING

Whip stitch medallion tog, work 2 rnd sc aroun the entire afghan, working ch 3 between each petal.

Basketweave Beauty

for beginner knitters

Two strands of thick chenille, large needles, and a simple knit and purl basketweave stitch are all you need to create this soft summer indulgence. The end result is a huge return on the relatively small investment of time and effort this one-weekend wonder requires. The "Basketweave Beauty," designed by Gitta Schrade, was first featured in the Winter '99/'00 issue of *Family Circle Easy Knitting*.

MATERIALS

- *Soft Bouclé* by Bernat®, 5oz/140g ball, each approx 255yd/232m (acrylic/ nylon)
  5 balls in #6703 ecru (MC)
- *Silky Soft*, 5oz/140g ball, each approx 285yd/260m (acrylic)
  1 ball in #374 royal (CC)
- Size 17 (12.75mm) circular needle, 24"/60cm long OR SIZE TO OBTAIN GAUGE
- Size G/6 (4.5mm) crochet hook
- Tapestry needle

FINISHED MEASUREMENTS

- 44" x 56"/112cm x 140cm

GAUGE

11 sts and 8 rows to 4"/10cm over pat st using size 17 (12.75mm) needles.
TAKE TIME TO CHECK YOUR GAUGE.

Note

Entire afghan is worked with 2 strands of MC held tog throughout.

AFGHAN

With 2 strands MC held tog, cast on 77 sts. **
(*) **Row 1(RS)** K11, *p11, k11; rep from * to end.
Row 2 P the purl-sts and k the knit-sts.
Rep these last 2 rows until 16 rows have been worked in total. (*)
Next row (RS) P11, *k11, p11; rep from * to end.
Row 2 K the knit sts and p the purl sts.
Rep these last 2 rows until 16 rows have been worked in total.**.
Rep from ** to ** 3 times more, then rep from (*) to (*) once more.
Bind off.

FINISHING

Using tapestry needle and 3 strands of CC, give afghan "Quilted Look", by working running st lines diagonal through all squares, then in opposite direction.
With crochet hook and 2 strands of MC, work 1 rnd sc around entire afghan.
Next rnd With CC, *sc in next 3 sts, sk 1 st, work 3 sc in next st, sk 1 st; rep from * around. Fasten off.

Portable Throw

for beginner knitters

Plump cables alternate with airy openwork in Ann Regis's weightless work of art. Surprisingly easy to knit, this light and elegant afghan features a seed-stitch border and fat, fluffy tassels. Worked with two strands of yarn and very large needles, the "Portable Throw" is deceptively simple to make. It was first featured in the Fall '94 issue of *Family Circle Easy Knitting*.

MATERIALS

- *Imagine* by Lion Brand Yarn Co., 2½oz skeins, each approx 222yd/200m (acrylic/mohair)
  6 skeins in #099 ecru (A)
  6 skeins #186 maize (B)
- Size 17 (12.75mm) circular needle, 24"/60cm OR SIZE TO OBTAIN GAUGE
- 1 Cable needle (cn)
- 1 Stitch markers
- Tassels (optional)
  2 skeins each in #099 ecru (A) and #186 maize (B)

FINISHED MEASUREMENTS

- 50" x 56"/127cm x 142.5cm

GAUGE

8 sts and 10 rows to 4"/10cm in St st using size 17 (12.75mm) needles and 2 strands of yarn held tog.
TAKE TIME TO CHECK YOUR GAUGE.

STITCHES

Seed stitch

Row 1 *K1, p1; rep from *. **Row 2** K the purl sts and p the knit sts. Rep row 2 for seed st pat.

Chevron and Feather

(multiple of 13 sts + 1 extra)
Row 1 (RS) *K1, yo, W, k2tog, ssk, k4, yo; rep from * to last st, k1. **Row 2** Purl. Rep rows 1-2 for chevron and feather pat.

16-st Back Cable Twist

P2, sl 6 sts to cable needle (cn), hold to back of work, k6, k6 from cn, p2.

Color pat

*14 rows A, 14 rows B; rep from *

Notes

1 Use 2 strands of A or B held tog.
2 Sl markers every row.

AFGHAN

With 2 strands of B held tog, cast on 126 sts. Work 7 rows in seed st. Change to 2 strands of A held tog.

Beg pats

Row 1 (RS) Cont seed st on 5 sts, place marker (pm), ssk, k4, yo, k1, pm, [p2, k12, p2, pm, work row 1 of chevron and feather pat over next 27 sts, pm] twice, p2, k12, p2, pm, k1, yo, k4, k2tog, pm, cont seed st on 5 sts.
Row 2 (WS) Cont seed st on 5 sts, p7, [k2, p12, k2, p27] twice, k2, p12, k2, p7, cont seed st on 5 sts.
Row 3 Rep row 1, working 16-st back cable twist between 2nd and 3rd, 4th and 5th, and 6th and 7th markers.

Row 4 Rep row 2. Rep rows 1 and 2, working 16-st back cable twist on row 17 and then every 14th row, AT SAME TIME, cont to work color pat as established, changing to B after 14 rows of A have been worked. When 5th stripe of A and 10 cable twists have been worked, end with a WS row. Change to B. Work 6 rows in seed st. Bind off loosely in pat. Piece measures approx 56"/142.5cm from beg.

Tassels

(Optional; make 4)

Cut a piece of cardboard 9"/23cm long or desired length. With I strand each A and B held tog, wrap yarn around cardboard 60 times or to desired thickness. Insert yarn and tie at top, leaving a long tail to secure to afghan. Cut strands at other edge. With separate strand, wrap tassel approx 1"/2.5cm from top. Attach 1 tassel to each corner, wrapping tail several times around corner.

By the Piece

From simple to sensational, these afghans span the seasons in any climate.

Snowflake Sensation

for intermediate knitters

Creamy white snowflakes dance across richly colored squares in this cozy winter must-have, designed by Cocoa Baker. A fleece backing, stitched on after crocheting the pieces together, makes this afghan extra-cuddly. It's the first thing family members will reach for after a chilly afternoon of skiing, skating, or snowman-making. The "Snowflake Sensation" afghan first appeared in the Winter '97/'98 issue of *Family Circle Easy Knitting*.

MATERIALS

■ *Madelaine* by Unger/JCA, 1¾oz/50g balls, each approx 93yd/85m
   (wool/ acrylic/nylon)
   9 balls #806 cream (E)
   5 balls each #811 blue (A), #817 green (B) , #813 burgundy (C), #814 orange (D)
■ Size 10½ (6.5mm) needles OR SIZE TO OBTAIN GAUGE
■ Crochet hook size H/5mm
■ 2yd/2m of polar fleece, approx 62"/158cm wide

FINISHED MEASUREMENTS

■ 51" x 51"/129.5cm x 129.5cm

GAUGE

31 sts and 33 rows to 8"/22cm square over chart pat, using size 10½ (6.5mm) needles. TAKE TIME TO CHECK GAUGE.

Note

When changing colors, carry yarns loosely across back of work.

THROW

With size 10½ (6.5mm) needles and A, cast on 31 sts. Work 3 rows St st. Beg Chart A
Next row (RS) K2, work 27 sts of Chart A, k2. Keeping first 2 sts and last 2 sts in St st, work

27 rows of chart. Work 3 rows St st with A. Bind off. Make 8 more squares in same manner. Make 9 squares each using Chart B (using B for MC), C (using C for MC) and D (using D for MC) (36 squares).

FINISHING

Block squares. With E, single crochet around each square. Crochet squares together in 6 rows of 6 squares. Crochet rows together. Cut polar fleece to fit back. Slip stitch in place.

Color key

□ MC	⊠ Cream (E)

CHART A

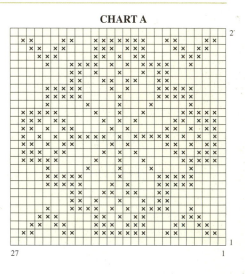

27   1

CHART B

27   1

CHART C

27   1

CHART D

27   1

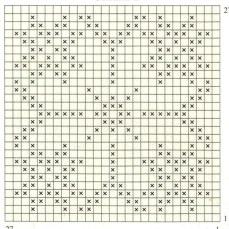

Home Sweet Home

for intermediate knitters

Home is where the heart is, and how better to embrace the values and comforts of your personal heaven than with this treasured keepsake? Delightful house motifs mingle with checkerboard-patterned squares in simple stockinette and seed stitches to create a patchwork look while heathered colors beckon all hearts homeward. The "Home Sweet Home" afghan first appeared in the Fall '96 issue of *Family Circle Easy Knitting*.

MATERIALS

■ *Galway Highland Heather* by Plymouth, 3½oz/100g, each approx 230yd/209m (wool)
8 hanks of #723 sage (A)
1 hank #12 cranberry (B)
1 hank or small amounts each of #13 purple (C), #1 cream (D),
#18 deep teal (E),#49 coral (F) and #60 gold (G)
■ Size 18 (4mm) needles OR SIZE TO OBTAIN GAUGE

FINISHED MEASUREMENTS

■ 70" x 56"/178.5cm x 142cm
(Each Square 8" x 8"/20.5cm x 20.5cm)

GAUGE

20 sts and 28 rows to 4"/10cm on size 8 (4mm) needles in St st.
TAKE TIME TO CHECK YOUR GAUGE.

STITCHES

Seed stitch

(Odd # of sts)
K1, p1 across end k1. Repeat row 1 for pat.

AFGHAN SQUARES

House Squares (Make 17)

With A cast on 41 sts work 4 rows in seed St. Next 4 rows Keeping a border of 3 seed sts (K1, p1, k1) at each side of work, work 2 rows St st, end with a WS row.

Beg chart

Row 1 Work 35 sts of Chart in St st, keeping a border of 3 seed sts each side. Cont in pat as established until row 48 of chart is worked. Work 4 rows seed st. Bind off.

Seed st and Stockinette squares (Make 18)

With A cast on 41 st. Work 4 rows seed st.
Row 5 (RS) K1,p1, k1, *k7, work 7 sts seed st * rep from * to last 3 sts, end k1, p1, k1.
Row 6 (WS) K1, p1, k1 *P7,Work 7 sts seed st; rep from * to last 3 sts, end k1, p1, k1. Keeping a border of 3 seed sts at each side of work.

Work row 5 and 6—4 more times (10 rows of pat completed).

Row 11 (RS) Work 3 sts seed st *7 sts seed st, k7 sts, rep from * to last 3 sts, work 3 in seed st.
Row 12 Work 3 sts seed st. *7 sts in seed st. 7 sts in p. rep from *to last 3 sts, work 3 sts in seed st. Rep rows 11 & 12, 4 more times (20 rows of pat completed). Rep rows 1-20 once, work rows 1-10. Work 4 rows seed st. Bind off.

FINISHING

Sew off all ends. Block squares to measurements. Sew squares together alternating one solid square with one house square.

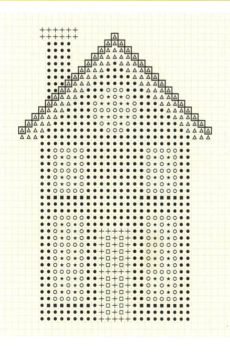

○ Cream   □ Coral
■ Deep Teal   △ Coral
★ Gold   ● Cranberry
+ Purple   ▲ Coral

Lighthouse Keeper

for intermediate knitters

Add a comforting beacon to a summer home with Gitta Schrade's bright and breezy afghan. Alternating lighthouse and seed-stitch squares are framed with garter stitch bands of bold contrasting colors. The "Lighthouse Keeper" afghan first appeared in the Spring/Summer '98 issue of *Family Circle Easy Knitting*.

MATERIALS
- *Canadiana* by Patons®, 3½oz/100g skeins, each approx 228yd/208m (acrylic)
  5 skeins each in #157 red (A) and #48 dk green (B)
  3 skeins in #33 navy (C)
  2 skeins in #138 lt blue (D)
  1 skein each in #32 royal (E), #47 med green (F) and #101 white (G)
- One pair each sizes 4, 5 and 6 (3.5mm, 3.75mm and 4mm) needles
  OR SIZE TO OBTAIN GAUGE
- Size 4 (3.5mm) circular needle 39"/100cm long (used back and forth)
- Stitch holder
- Tapestry needle

FINISHED MEASUREMENTS
- 52" x 62"/132cm x 158cm

GAUGES
20 sts and 26 rows to 4"/10cm over St st using size 6 (4mm) needles.
20 sts and 33 rows to 4"/10cm over Seed st using size 5 (3.75mm) needles.
TAKE TIME TO CHECK YOUR GAUGES.

STITCHES USED
Seed stitch
Row 1 (RS) *K1, p1; rep from *.
Row 2 (WS) P the knit sts and k the purl sts.
Rep row 2 for seed st.

AFGHAN
Lighthouse squares
(Make 15)
With size 6 (4mm) needles and F, cast on 40 sts. Work in St st and 52 rows of chart. Bind off. Birds are embroidered after pieces are knit.

Seed st squares
(Make 15)
With size 5 (3.75mm) needles and A, cast on 40 sts. Work in Seed st for 66 rows. Bind off.

Short grid panels
(Using C make 4; using B make 5)
With size 4 (3.5mm) needles and required color, cast on 40 sts. Work in garter st for 20 rows. Bind off.

Long grid panels
(Using C make 10; using B make 10)
With size 4 (3.5mm) needles and required color, cast on 90 sts. Work in garter st for 20 rows. Bind off.

FINISHING
With tapestry needle and G, duplicate st birds on Lighthouse squares. Block Lighthouse squares. Sew pieces tog foll placement diagram.

BORDER
With circular needle and B, pick up and k 238 sts along bottom edge of afghan. Work in garter st for 22 rows, AT SAME TIME, inc 1 st each side every RS row to shape edges. Bind off in C, place last loop on holder, do not break yarn. Pick up and k 288 sts along side edge of afghan. Work in garter st for 22 rows, AT SAME TIME, inc 1 st each side every RS row to shape edges. Sew corner seam. Using st from holder and C, work 1 st, cont to bind off. Work rem sides to match. With tapestry needle and C, embroider chain stitches above corner seams.

(See charts on page 132)

Rhapsody in Blue

for intermediate knitters

Part crazy quilt, part sampler afghan: Get inspired and explore the interesting stitch patterns featured in this beautiful afghan in tranquil hues of blue. Join squares together, then attach a fabric back and edge to complete the look. The "Rhapsody in Blue" afghan first appeared in the Spring/Summer '01 issue of *Family Circle Easy Knitting*.

MATERIALS

- *Décor* by Patons®, 3oz/100g balls, each approx 210yd/192m (acrylic/wool)
  3 balls each in #1649 periwinkle, #1641 lilac, #1642 med blue and #1643 navy
- One pair size 7 (4.5mm) needles OR SIZE TO OBTAIN GAUGE
- 2yd/1.85m fabric for lining (optional)
- Cable needle

FINISHED MEASUREMENTS

- 40" x 60"/101.5cm x 152cm (without fabric border)

GAUGES

20 sts and 28 rows to 4"/10cm over St st using size 7 (4.5mm) needles.
Each block measures approx 8"/20.5cm wide by 10"/25.5cm long using size 7 (4.5mm) needles.
TAKE TIME TO CHECK YOUR GAUGE.

STITCHES USED

1 selvage st
Work st in garter st (k every row). Work 1 selvage st each side of every block.
2-st Right Purl Cable (RPC)
Sl 1 st to cn and hold to back, k1, p1 from cn.
2-st Left Purl Cable (LPC)
Sl 1 st to cn and hold to front, p1, k1 from cn.
4-st Right Cable (RC)
Sl 2 sts to cn and hold to back, k2, k2 from cn.
4-st Left Cable (LC)
Sl 2 sts to cn and hold to front, k2, k2 from cn.

BLOCKS

Make 3 blocks of each of the foll 10 pat sts, working 7 blocks in each of 2 colors and 8 blocks in each of the other 2 colors, for a total of 30 blocks.

PATTERN 1

Cast on 42 sts.
Row 1 (RS) 1 selvage st, *p4, k8; rep from *, end p4, 1 selvage st.
Rows 2-4 K the knit sts and p the purl sts.
Row 5 1 selvage st, *p4, 4-st RC, 4-st LC; rep from *, end p4, 1 selvage st.
Row 6 Rep row 2.
Rep rows 1-6 for square 1 until piece measures 10"/25.5cm. Bind off.

PATTERN 2

Cast on 42 sts.
Row 1 (RS) Knit.
Row 2 Purl.
Row 3 1 selvage st, *k2, yo, k2tog; rep from *, end 1 selvage st.
Row 4 Purl, including yo sts.
Row 5 Knit.
Row 6 Purl.
Row 7 1 selvage st, *yo, k2tog, k2; rep from *, end 1 selvage st.
Row 8 Rep row 4.
Rep rows 1-8 for square 2 until piece measures 10"/25.5cm. Bind off.

PATTERN 3

Cast on 46 sts.

Preparation row (WS) 1 selvage st, *k2, p; rep from *, end k2, 1 selvage st.
Row 1 (RS) 1 selvage st, *P2, 2-st LPC, 2-st RPC; rep from *, end p2, 1 selvage st.
Rows 2 and 4 K the knit sts and p the purl sts.
Row 3 1 selvage st, *p2, 2-st RPC, 2-st LPC; rep from *, end p2, 1 selvage st.
Rep rows 1-4 for square 3 until piece measures 10"/25.5cm. Bind off.

PATTERN 4

Cast on 42 sts.
Rows 1 and 5 (RS) 1 selvage st, p5, k1 tbl, p5, k18, p5, k1 tbl, p5, 1 selvage st.
Rows 2, 4, 6 and 8 K the knit sts and p the purl sts.
Row 3 1 selvage st, p5, k1 tbl, p5, [sl 3 sts to cn and hold to back, k3, k3 from cn] 3 times, p5, k1 tbl, p5, 1 selvage st.
Row 7 1 selvage st, p5, k1 tbl, p5, k3, [sl 3 sts to cn and hold to front, k3, k3 from cn] twice, k3, p5, k1 tbl, p5, 1 selvage st.
Rep rows 1-8 for square 4 until piece measures 10"/25.5cm. Bind off.

PATTERN 5

Cast on 41 sts.
Row 1 1 selvage st, *yo, SKP, k5, k2tog, yo, k1; rep from * to end.

(Continued on page 133)

Autumn Splendor

for intermediate knitters

Comfort, style and fabulous fall tones abound in this striking leaf-motif afghan. Each leaf is knit separately in stockinette and shaped with simple decreases. The knitted leaves are then pieced together to create the afghan. "Autumn Splendor" first appeared in the Winter '98/'99 issue of *Family Circle Easy Knitting*.

MATERIALS

- *TLC*® by Coats & Clark, 5oz/140g, each approx 253yd/236m (100% Acrylic with Bounce-Back fibers®)
  2 skeins each in #5919 red, #5288 rust, #5342 brown, #5644 gold, #5660 lt green, #5666 dk green, #5339 tan and #5335 sand
- One pair size 9 (5.5mm) needles OR SIZE TO OBTAIN GAUGE

FINISHED MEASUREMENTS

- 54" x 60"/137cm x 152cm

GAUGE

16 sts and 24 rows to 4"/10cm over leaf pat using size 9 (5.5mm) needles.
TAKE TIME TO CHECK YOUR GAUGE.

STITCHES USED

Leaf Pattern

Row 1 K13, SKP, pm, k to end.
Row 2 K1, p to 2 sts before marker, p2tog, sl marker, p to last st, k1.
Row 3 K to 2 sts before marker, SKP, sl marker

k to end. Rep last 2 rows until 4 sts rem.
Next row K1, SKP, k1.
Next row P3tog. Fasten off.

Leaves

(Make 170)
Cast on 30 sts. Work in leaf pat. Make 21 of each color plus 2 extra in any color.

Right Half Leaves

(Make 10 in any color)
Cast on 15 sts.
Row 1 K to last 3 sts, SKP, k1.
Row 2 K1, p to last st, k1.
Rep these 2 rows until 2 sts rem.
Next row P2tog. Fasten off.

Left Half Leaves

(Make 10 in any color)
Cast on 15 sts.
Row 1 Knit.
Row 2 K1, p to last 3 sts, p2tog, k1.
Rep these 2 rows until 3 sts rem.
Next row P3tog. Fasten off.

FINISHING

Sew 17 leaves tog alternating points in opposite direction to make one row. Sew 10 rows tog. Sew half leaves to sides of afghan.

Warm and Wooly

for intermediate knitters

This irresistible afghan, designed by Gitta Schrade, features a fenced-in flock of playfully plump intarsia sheep, guarded by dutiful dogs. Knit in natural shades of heathered yarn, the "Warm and Wooly" afghan first appeared in the Fall '99 issue of *Family Circle Easy Knitting*.

MATERIALS

- *Tussock Chunky* 14-Ply by Naturally/S.R. Kertzer, Ltd., 3¹⁄₂oz/100g skeins, each approx 124yd/115m (wool)
  5 skeins each in #561 natural tweed (A) and #562 brown tweed (B)
- *Naturally* 14-Ply by Naturally/S.R. Kertzer, Ltd., 3¹⁄₂oz/100g skeins, each approx 130yd/120m (wool)
  2 skeins each in #550 ecru (C) and #554 grey (H)
  7 skeins in #551 natural (D),
  1 skein each in #552 lt brown (E) and #558 brown (G)
  3 skeins in #553 med brown (F)
- One pair size10 (6mm) needles OR SIZE TO OBTAIN GAUGE
- Crochet hook size E/4 (3.5mm)
- Tapestry needle

FINISHED MEASUREMENTS

- 48" x 72"/122cm x 183cm

GAUGE

46 sts and 60 rows (one square) to 12"/30.5cm over chart pat using size 10 (6mm) needles.
TAKE TIME TO CHECK YOUR GAUGE.

AFGHAN

Squares

(Make 15)

Make squares foll placement diagram. The numbers on the diagram refer to the chart number. Use the corresponding colors in each chart. For example, 2 in a circle refers to chart 2, using the colors indicated in the circle. With size 10 (6mm) needles and indicated color, cast on 46 sts. Work 60 rows of chart. Bind off.

FINISHING

Block squares. Sew pieces tog foll placement diagram.

BORDER

(Make 2 short and 2 long pieces)
With size 10 (6mm) needles and D, cast on 21 sts. K 4 rows.
Row 1 (RS) With F, knit.
Row 2 K8, yo, k1, yo, k5, yo, k1, yo, k6.
Row 3 With D, k6, sl 2 (drop yo's), k4, sl 2 (drop yo's), k7.
Rows 4 and 6 K7, sl 2 wyif, k4, sl 2 wyif, k6.
Row 5 K6, sl 2 wyib, k4, sl 2 wyib, k7. With F, k 2 rows. Work 68 rows of Chart 5. Rep rows 1-6 until piece measures 5"/13cm more than edge of afghan. With F, k 2 rows. With D, k 3 rows. Bind off. With tapestry needle and E, embroider outline along C-sections. Sew border in place. With crochet hook and D, work 2 rnds sc around entire afghan.

Placement Diagram

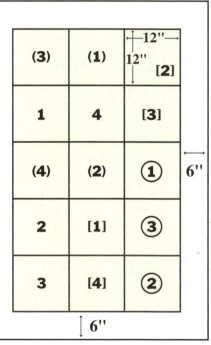

(See charts on page 134)

Sophisticated Sampler

for intermediate knitters

From zigzags and basketweave to bobbles and cables, Lila P. Chin's classic, cream-colored afghan is a knitted gallery of artistic stitches. Worked in squares featuring six different stitch patterns, this elegant collection combines textural finesse with cozy comfort. The "Sophisticated Sampler" first appeared in the Winter '98/'99 issue of *Family Circle Easy Knitting*.

MATERIALS

- *Jiffy®* by Lion Brand Yarn Co., 3oz/85g skeins, each approx 135yd/124m (acrylic) 21 skeins in #99 off white
- One pair size 10 (6mm) needles OR SIZE TO OBTAIN GAUGE
- Cable needle
- Tapestry needle
- Size H/8 crochet hook
- 16" x 16"/40.5cm x 40.5cm pillow form

FINISHED MEASUREMENTS

Throw
- 48" x 64"/122cm x 162.5cm

Pillows
- 16" x 16"/40cm x 40cm

GAUGE

15 sts and 20 rows to 4"/10cm over St st using size 10 (6mm) needles.
TAKE TIME TO CHECK YOUR GAUGE.

Note

Afghan is made in squares that are sewn tog foll afghan square diagram.

STITCHES USED

Bobble
(K1, p1, k1, p1, k1) in the same st. Turn, p5, turn. Pass 2nd, 3rd, 4th and 5th sts one at a time over first st.

6-st LC
Sl 3 sts to cn and hold to front, k3, k3 from cn.

AFGHAN

Square 1 (Make 8)
Cast on 30 sts and work chart square 1, working 10-st rep 3 times. Cont foll chart until piece measures 8"/20cm from beg. Bind off.

Square 2
(Make 8)
Cast on 28 sts and beg chart square 2, working 6-st rep 4 times, then last 4 sts once. Cont foll chart until piece measures 8"/20cm from beg. Bind off.

Square 3
(Make 8)
Cast on 34 sts and beg chart square 3, working 10-st rep 3 times, then last 4 sts once. Cont chart until piece measures 8"/20cm from beg. Bind off.

Square 4
(Make 8)
Cast on 29 sts and beg chart square 4, work first 2 sts once, then 6-st rep 4 times, then last 3 sts once. Cont to work chart until piece measures 8"/20cm from beg. Bind off.

Square 5
(Make 8)
Cast on 30 sts and beg chart square 5, work first st once, then 8-st rep 3 times, then last 5 sts once. Cont foll chart until piece measures 8"/20cm from beg. Bind off.

Square 6
(Make 8)
Cast on 32 sts and beg chart square 6, work first 2 sts once, then 6-st rep 5 times. Cont chart until piece measures 8"/20cm from beg. Bind off.

FINISHING

Block pieces lightly. Using afghan square diagram, sew squares tog. Work sc evenly around outside edge. Make tassels and sew to corners.

PILLOWS

Version 1
Make 2 of each of the foll squares: 1, 3, 5, 6.
Version 2
Make 2 of each of the foll squares: 2, 3, 4, 6.

FINISHING

Foll pillow square diagram and sew squares tog. Sew 3 seams. Insert pillow form. Sew last seam. Make tassels and sew to corners.

(See charts on page 135)

Triangle Treasure

for intermediate knitters

Basic geometry takes on a new softness and warmth with this take-anywhere afghan. Garter-stitch triangles in neutral and bright shades tumble together into eye-pleasing combinations to form squares that, when sewn together and finished with a simple single crochet border, build an eye-catching accessory for any room. The "Triangle Treasure" first appeared in the Fall '95 issue of *Family Circle Easy Knitting.*

MATERIALS
- *Cascade* by Hayfield/Cascade 3½oz/100g, each approx 220yd/201m (100% Monsanto® acrylic)
  4 skeins each in #8895 Crimson, #8021 Beige, #11/4001 Grey, #10/2417 Green, #8339 Blue, #8240 Purple
- One pair size 6 (4mm) needles OR SIZE TO OBTAIN GAUGE
- Size F/5 (4mm) crochet hook

FINISHED MEASUREMENTS
- 45½" x 65"/188cm x 168cm

GAUGE
One square (two triangles sewed tog) to 6½"/16.5cm in size 6 (4mm) needles in garter st. TAKE TIME TO CHECK YOUR GAUGE.

Note
Triangles are made separately and sewn tog afterwards.

TRIANGLE S
Cast on 35 sts and work in garter st (k every row), dec 1 st at beg of every RS row until there are 3 sts. K3tog and fasten off.

AFGHAN
Make 140 traingles as foll
24 in Grey
24 in Crimson
23 in Beige
23 in Green
23 in Purple
23 in Blue

FINISHING
Sew triangles tog foll diagram for placement.

EDGING
With crochet hook and grey, work 1 rnd sc evenly around entire outside edge of afghan.

Winter Wonderland

for intermediate knitters

Bring in the holiday season with this bright blanket, emblazoned with trees, stars, and snowflakes arranged in a patchwork between bright red textured squares. The winter motifs are worked in single crochet in a color block technique, while the red squares combine single and triple crochet for a bobbled effect. The "Winter Wonderland" afghan first appeared in the Fall '96 issue of *Family Circle Easy Knitting*.

MATERIALS

- *Classic Wool* by Patons®, 3½oz/100g, each approx 223yd/204m (wool)
  11 skeins of #230 red (MC)
  3 skeins each of #201 winter white (A), #223 royal blue (B), #204 gold (C)
  2 skeins of #221 green (D)
- Size #7/8 (5mm) crochet hook OR SIZE TO OBTAIN GAUGE
- Size #7 (4.5mm) knitting needles OR SIZE TO OBTAIN GAUGE

FINISHED MEASUREMENTS

Afghan
- 46 x 64"/117 x 162.5 cm

Pillow
- 12" x 12"/30.5cm x 30.5cm

CROCHET INSTRUCTIONS

GAUGE

14 sts and 14 rows to 4"/10 cm with #7/8 (5mm) hook. Each afghan square should measure 9"/23cm square.

Note

1 When working squares, do not strand across rows, use separate balls (Color block technique). Work the last st until 2 loops remain on hook, then draw new color through 2 loops to complete st.
2 Read charts from right to left on RS rows and from left to right on WS rows.

STITCHES

Sc Single crochet.
Tr Triple crochet.

AFGHAN

Star square
(Make 7)

With B, ch 32. 1st row: (RS). Sc in 2nd ch from hook. Sc in each ch across— 31 sc. Ch 1 at end of this and every row. (1st row of Star Chart is complete). Turn. Cont working chart to end. Fasten off.

Tree square
(Make 6)

With A, Ch 32. 1st row (RS) Sc in 2nd ch from hook. Sc in each ch across—31 sc. Ch 1 at end of this and every row. Turn. Work tree chart to end as for star chart.

Snowflake square c
(Make 4)

With B, ch 32.

1st row (RS) Sc in 2nd ch form hook. Sc in each ch acros—31 sc. Ch 1. Ch 1 at end of this and every row. Turn. Work snowflake chart to end as for star chart.

Solid color square
(Make 18)

With MC, ch 32. **1st row (RS).** Sc in 2nd ch from hook, sc in each ch across—31 sc. Ch 1 at end of this and every row. Turn. **2nd row** Sc in first sc. *Tr in next sc, sc in next sc. Rep from * to end. **3rd row** Sc in first st and each st to end. **4th row** Sc in each of first 2 sc. *Tr in next sc. Sc in next sc. Rep from * to last sc. Sc in last sc. **5th row** Rep row 3. Rep rows 2—5 6 times, rows 2—3 until square measures 12"/30.5cm. Fasten off.

FINISHING

With MC single crochet squares together: Alternate patterned squares with solid squares. With D, sc around afghan once. Change to B, sc around once, fasten off.

PILLOW

Complete one charted square. Single crochet around square in contrasting color for 1"/2.5cm, change to main background color of square and single crochet until each side of square measures 12"/30.5cm. Back of pillow: With MC, make one solid color square. Sc finished square with MC, until measures same as charted square. Sew or sc 3 sides together, insert pillow form, sew or sc 4th side.

KNIT INSTRUCTIONS

FINISHED MEASUREMENTS

Afghan
- 42" x 60"/ 106.5cm x 152.5cm

Pillow
- 12" x 12"/30.5cm x 30.5cm

GAUGE

20 sts and 26 rows to 4"/10cm over St st

using size 7 (4.5mm) needles
TAKE TIME TO CHECK YOUR GAUGE.

STITCHES USED

St st
K1 RS, p1 WS row.

DOUBLE SEED
(over even # of sts)
Row 1-2 K2, p2 across. Rows 3-4 P2, k2 across.

Note
Read charts from right to left on RS rows and from left to right and WS rows.

AFGHAN
For afghan, work center of chart, omitting borders (center 40 sts, starting on 13th row).

Solid color squares
(Double seed st-make 18)
With MC cast on 40sts. Work in double seed until piece measures 8"/20cm. Bind off all sts.

Star squares
(Make 7)
With B, cast on 40sts. Follow Star chart in St st through row 68. Bind off all sts.

Tree squares
(Make 6)

With A, cast on 40 sts. Work snowflakes chart as for star square.

FINISHING
Same as for crocheted afghan.

PILLOW
Complete one charted square with all 60 sts and work in double seed until piece measurement same as charted square. Sew or sc 3 sides together, insert pillow form, sew or sc 4th side.

KNIT CHARTS

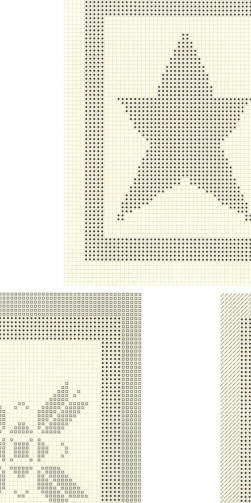

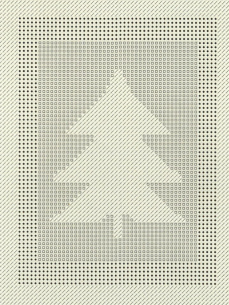

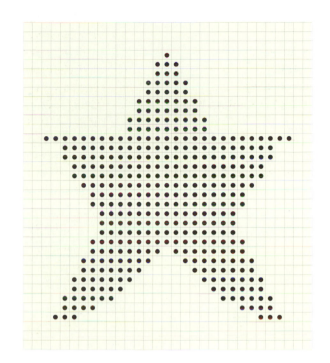

CROCHET CHARTS

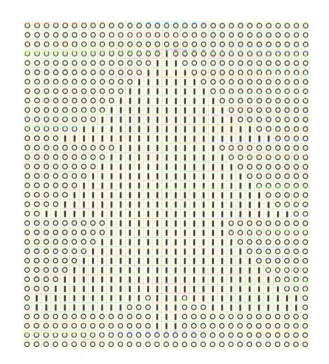

On the Whole

Comfortable creations, rich in color and texture, accent the home all year round.

Lovely Lace
for intermediate knitters

Nothing adds a soft, feminine touch to a room like lace—and what could be more luxurious than a lace blanket worked in the softest chenille? This afghan, drenched in a hydrangea hue, is knit in an eyelet stitch that forms an overall shell pattern. A thick fringe adds a luxurious finish. The "Lovely Lace" afghan first appeared in the Spring/Summer '99 issue of *Family Circle Easy Knitting*.

MATERIALS
■ *Cotton Chenille* by Crystal Palace Yarns, 1³/₄oz/ 50g balls, each approx 98yd/89m (cotton)
  15 balls in #1404 lavender (A)
■ Size 7 (4.5mm) circular needle, 29"/74cm long OR SIZE TO OBTAIN GAUGE
■ Size H/8 (5mm) crochet hook
■ Stitch markers

FINISHED MEASUREMENTS
■ 36¹/₂" x 53¹/₂"/93cm x 136cm

GAUGE
20 sts and 28 rows to 4"/10cm over pat st using size 7 (4.5mm) needles.
TAKE TIME TO CHECK YOUR GAUGE.

SHELL LACE PATTERN
Row 1 (RS) K2tog, *k5, yo, k1, yo, k2, SK2P; rep from * to last 10 sts, end k5, yo, k1, yo, k2, ssk.
Row 2 and all WS rows Purl.
Row 3 K2tog, *k4, yo, k3, yo, k1, SK2P; rep from * to last 10 sts, end k4, yo, k3, yo, k1, ssk.
Row 5 K2tog, *k3, yo, k5, yo, SK2P; rep from * to last 10 sts, end k3, yo, k5, yo, ssk.
Row 7 K2tog, *k2, yo, k1, yo, k5, SK2P; rep from * to last 10 sts, end k2, yo, k1, yo, k5, ssk.

Row 9 K2tog, *k1, yo, k3, yo, k4, SK2P; rep from * to last 10 sts, end k1, yo, k3, yo, k4, ssk.
Row 11 K2tog, *yo, k5, yo, k3, SK2P; rep from * to last 10 sts, end k5, yo, k3, ssk.
Row 12 Purl.
Rep rows 1-12 for shell lace pat.

THROW
Loosely cast on 183 sts.
Beg border
Rows 1 and 3 K1, *p1, k1; rep from * to end.
Rows 2 and 4 P1, *k1, p1; rep from * to end.
Beg shell lace pat
Row 1 K1, p1, k1, pm, work row 1 of shell lace pat to last 3 sts, pm, k1, p1, k1.
Row 2 P1, k1, p1, work row 2 of shell lace pat to 2nd marker, p1, k1, p1.
Cont in pat as established until piece measures

53"/135cm from beg, end with a RS row and inc 1 st in center—183 sts.

BORDER
Rows 1 and 3 K1, *p1, k1; rep from * to end.
Rows 2 and 4 P1, *k1, p1; rep from * to end.
Bind off loosely in ribbing.

FINISHING
Fringe
Cut two 12"/30.5cm long strands. Hold tog and fold in half. With crochet hook, draw center of strand through first st of cast-on edge, forming a lp. Pull ends through lp. Cont as established in every other st of cast-on and bound-off edges. Trim even if necessary. Steam lightly.

Mitered Magic
for intermediate knitters

Accent a favorite room with this cozy country charmer. Mitered corners and a medley of eye-catching colors lend to the dynamics of this splendid creation by Uyvonne Bigham. The "Mitered Magic" afghan first appeared in the Winter '97/'98 issue of *Family Circle Easy Knitting*.

MATERIALS

■ *Encore* by Plymouth 3½oz/100g skeins, each approx 200yd/184m (acrylic/wool)
 5 skeins #7002 lavender multi (MC)
 2 skeins each in #194 lt. grey (A), #433 heather mauve (B), #355 heather plum (C), #180 rose (D), #504 purple (E), #517 blue (F) and #389 dk grey (G)
■ One pair size 9 (5.5mm) needles OR SIZE TO OBTAIN GAUGE
■ Size 9 (5.5mm) circular needle, 29"/75cm long
■ Stitch markers

FINISHED MEASUREMENTS

■ 42" x 62"/106cm x 157cm

GAUGE

18 sts and 22 rows to 4"/10cm over St st using size 9 (5.5mm) needles.
TAKE TIME TO CHECK GAUGE.

COLOR KEY FOR DIAMONDS

Diamond A CC is A. Diamond B CC is B. Diamond C CC is C. Diamond D CC is D. Diamond E CC is E. Diamond F CC is F. Diamond G CC is G.

DIAMOND

Cast on 40 sts with MC (or pick up and k40).
Rows 1 and 3 (WS) With MC, knit.
Row 2 With MC, k18, k2tog, place marker (pm), SKP, k to end.
Row 4 With CC, k to 2 sts before marker, k2tog, sl marker, SKP, k to end.
Row 5 With CC, purl.
Row 6 With CC, k2, *yo, k2tog, k1*, rep between *s to marker, end last rep k2tog instead of k1; SKP, rep between *s to last st, k1.
Row 7 With CC, purl.
Row 8 With MC, rep row 4.

Row 9 With MC, knit.
Rep rows 4-9 for 4 times more, then rep rows 4 and 5 until 1 st rem. Fasten off.

HALF DIAMOND (RIGHT SIDE)

With RS facing, pick up and k20 sts along right edge of diamond. Work as for Diamond, but work sts after the marker only.

HALF DIAMOND (LEFT SIDE)

With RS facing, pick up and k20 sts along left edge diamond. Work as for Diamond, but work sts before marker only.

THROW

With straight needles, work 6 separate diamonds as foll: A, B, C, D, A, B. Foll diagram from right to left, join Diamonds B and A as foll: with RS facing and MC, pick up and k20 sts along left edge of B and 20 sts along right edge of A—40 sts. Work Diamond C. Join Diamonds A and D in same way (working Diamond G). Cont to join diamonds in this way, foll diagram. Work Half diamond (left side) C on rem edge of Diamond A. Work Half diamond (right side) D on rem edge of Diamond B.

Cont to work diamonds and half diamonds foll diagram. Rep chart sequence until piece measures 62"/106cm. End with sequence C, D, E, F, A, C.

FINISHING

With RS facing, straight needles and MC, foll diagram from right to left, pick up and k20 sts along right edge of Diamond C. K 3 rows. Bind off. *Pick up and k22 sts along left edge of diamond (including garter band), pm, then pick up and k20 sts along next diamond edge—42 sts. K 3 rows, dec 1 st at marker on rows 1 and 2: rep from * 4 times more. Pick up and k22 sts along rem edge of Diamond C. K 3 rows. Bind off. With RS facing, circular needle and MC, pick up and k 248 sts along each side edge. Knit 3 rows. Bind off.

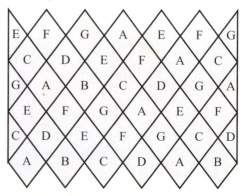

Indian Wrap
for intermediate knitters

Embrace color and culture with the perfect family heirloom. Inspired by Native American weavings, Mary Jane Protus's serape-style blanket boasts intricate motifs, vibrant colorwork, and a backward single-crochet border. The "Indian Wrap" afghan first appeared in the Fall '00 issue of *Family Circle Easy Knitting*.

MATERIALS
- *Lopi* ® by Reynolds/JCA, 3¹/₂oz/100g balls, each approx 110yd/101m (wool)
  - 5 balls each in #0051 natural (MC) and #0054 black (A)
  - 2 balls each in #0078 red (B), #0070 yellow (C) and #0121 teal (D)
- Size 10 (6mm) circular needle, 40"/100cm long OR SIZE TO OBTAIN GAUGE
- Size H/8 (5mm) crochet hook

FINISHED MEASUREMENTS
- 38" x 58"/96.5cm x 147cm

GAUGE
15 sts and 19 rows to 4"/10cm over St st and chart pat using 10 (6mm) needles. TAKE TIME TO CHECK YOUR GAUGE.

Note
If desired, small areas of color can be worked in Duplicate st after piece is knit.

AFGHAN
With MC, cast on 142 sts. Work 2 rows St st.
Beg chart
Row 1 (RS) Work first st of chart, work 28-st rep 5 times, work last st of chart. Cont in pat as established until 50 rows have been worked 5 times, then work rows 1-23 once more. Work 2 rows MC. Bind off.

FINISHING
Block to measurements.

EDGING
Rnd 1 (RS) With RS facing, MC and crochet hook, join yarn at one corner, work sc, ch 1, sc in same sp, ch 1, *skip a sp (that equals ch 1, sc), sc in next sp, ch 1; rep from * to next corner, in corner work [sc, ch 1, sc]; cont in this way around all sides. Fasten off.
Rnd 2 Join A in ch-1 sp at corner and work backwards sc (from left to right) into each ch-1 sp evenly around all sides and corners, end with sl st to first st. Fasten off.

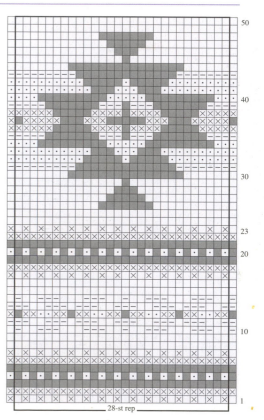

Color Key
- ☐ Natural (MC)
- ■ Black (A)
- ☒ Red (B)
- · Yellow (C)
- — Teal (D)

On the Whole

Stripe it Rich

for intermediate knitters

Jewel-toned stripes, some with purled ridges, add subtle texture to a bright, playful throw. Designed by Barbara Fimbel, this sporty afghan is worked with three strands in basic stockinette for a quick and easy knit. The "Stripe it Rich" afghan first appeared in the Winter '99/'00 issue of *Family Circle Easy Knitting*.

MATERIALS
■ *Wintuck* by Caron, 3¹⁄₂ oz/50g skein, each approx 208yd/192m (100% Acrilan® Acrylic)
   3 skeins each in #3048 deep red (A) and #3030 royal (C)
   2 skeins each in #3254 sky (B), #3256 yellow (D), #3044 brown (E), #3094 lilac (F), #3253 lt teal (G), #3081 violet (H), #3010 fir (I) and #3002 off white (J)
■ Size 13 (9mm) circular needle OR SIZE TO OBTAIN GAUGE
■ Size K/10 (7mm) crochet hook

FINISHED MEASUREMENTS
■ 55" x 64"/139.5cm x 162.5cm

GAUGE
12 sts and 16 rows to 4"/10cm over St st using size 13 (9mm) needles.
TAKE TIME TO CHECK YOUR GAUGE.

Note
Work with 2 strands of yarn held tog throughout.

AFGHAN
With A, cast on 162 sts. Work in St st as foll: *4 rows A, 2 rows B. K 2 rows C.
Cont in St st as foll: 2 rows D, 4 rows E, 2 rows F, 2 rows G, 2 rows H, 4 rows I, 2 rows J, 2 rows A, 4 rows B. K 2 rows C.
Cont in St st as foll: 4 rows D, 2 rows E, 4 rows F, 2 rows G, 4 rows H, 2 rows I, 4 rows J; rep from * 3times more.
Work 4 rows A. Bind off.

FINISHING
With C, work 1 row sc around outside edge working 3 sc in each corner. Working in back lp only, work sc in each sc, and 2 sc, ch 1, 2 sc in each corner. Fasten off.

Checkered Charm

for intermediate knitters

Couple old-fashioned checks with fresh color and sumptuous texture for a vintage-inspired afghan rich in tradition. Barbara Fimbel's simple fleece-backed throw knits in a flash on big needles. The "Checkered Charm" afghan first appeared in the Winter '99/'00 issue of *Family Circle Easy Knitting*.

MATERIALS

■ *Melody* by Patons®, 3½ oz/100g balls, each approx 85yd/78m
(100% Acrilan® Acrylic)
7 balls in #902 white (MC)
6 balls in #920 red (CC)
■ Size 13 (9mm) circular needle, 40"/100cm long OR SIZE TO OBTAIN GAUGE
■ 1½yd/1.4m polar fleece, 60"/150cm wide

FINISHED MEASUREMENTS

■ 54" x 60"/137cm x 152.5cm

GAUGE

10 sts and 10 rows to 4"/10cm over checkerboard pat using size 13 (9mm) needles. TAKE TIME TO CHECK YOUR GAUGE.

SEED STITCH

Row 1 (RS) *K1, p1; rep from * to end.
Row 2 K the purl sts and p the knit sts.
Rep row 2 for seed st.

Checkerboard pat

(Over 78 sts)
Rows 1 and 2 [2 CC, 2 MC] 19 times, 2 CC.
Rows 3 and 4 [2 MC, 2 CC] 19 times, 2 MC.
Rep rows 1-4 for checkboard pat.

AFGHAN

With CC, cast on 124 sts. Work in seed st for 7 rows.
Row 8 (WS) Work 7 sts seed st, p to last 7 sts, work 7 sts seed st.
Row 9 (RS) Work 7 sts seed st, join MC and work 110 sts in St st, join 2nd ball of CC and work 7 sts seed st. Cont in pat as established for 5 rows more.

Next row Work 7 sts in seed st with CC, k4 MC, [k2 CC, k2 MC] 25 times, k2 CC, k4 MC, work 7 sts in seed st with CC.
Next row Work St st, matching colors.
Next 2 rows Work 7 sts seed st with CC, work 110 sts in St st with MC, work 7 sts in seed st with CC.
Next 2 rows Work 7 sts seed st with CC, work110 in St st as foll: 4 MC, 2 CC, 98 MC, 2 CC, 4 MC, work 7 sts in seed st with CC.
Next 2 rows Work 7 sts seed st with CC, work 110 in St st with MC, work 7 sts in seed st with CC.
Rep last 4 rows once more.

Next 2 rows Work 7 sts in seed st with CC, work in St st as foll: 4 MC, 2 CC, 10 MC, rows 1 and 2 of checkerboard pat over78 sts, 10 MC, 2 CC, 4 MC; work 7 sts in seed st with CC.
Next 2 rows Work 7 sts in seed st with CC, work in St st as foll: 16 MC, rows 3 and 4 of checkerboard pat over 78 sts, 16 MC; 7 sts in seed st with CC.
Rep last 4 rows 26 times more.

Next 2 rows Work 7 sts in seed st with CC, work in St st as foll: 4 MC, 2 CC, 10 MC, rows 1 and 2 of checkerboard pat over 78 sts, 10 MC, 2 CC, 4 MC; work 7 sts in seed st with CC.

Next 2 rows Work 7 sts in seed st with CC, work 110 sts in St st with MC, 7 sts in seed st with CC.
Next 2 rows Work 7 sts seed st with CC, work 110 in St st as foll: 4 MC, 2 CC, 98 MC, 2 CC, 4 MC, work 7 sts in seed st with CC.
Rep last 4 rows once more.

Next 2 rows Work 7 sts in seed st with CC, work 110 sts in St st with MC, 7 sts in seed st with CC.

Next row Work 7 sts in seed st with CC, k4 MC, [k2 CC, k2 MC] 25 times, k2 CC, k4 MC, work 7 sts in seed st with CC.
Next 6 rows Work 7 sts in seed st with CC, work 110 sts in St st with MC, 7 sts in seed st with CC.

Next row Work 7 sts in seed st with CC, work 110 sts in St st with CC, 7 sts in seed st with CC. Work all sts in seed st with CC for 7 rows more. Bind off.

FINISHING

Block to measurements. Cut polar fleece to 52" x 58"/132cm x 147.5cm and sew to back of afghan.

Cream of the Crop

for intermediate knitters

This creamy chill-chaser offers luxury and sophistication to any room. Edged in crochet bobbles, this classic style features a ribbed rope detail that combines chunky cables with slanted rib panels. The "Cream of the Crop" afghan first appeared in the Winter '99/'00 issue of *Family Circle Easy Knitting*.

MATERIALS

■ *Waterspun* by Classic Elite Yarns, 1¾oz/50g skeins, each approx 137yd/126m (wool)
   20 skeins in #5016 natural
■ Size 8 (5mm) circular needle OR SIZE TO OBTAIN GAUGE
■ Size G/6 (4.5mm) crochet hook
■ Cable needle

FINISHED MEASUREMENTS

■ 40" x 64"/101.5 cm x 162.5cm

GAUGE

21 sts and 27 rows to 4"/10cm over charts 1 or 3 using size 8 (5mm) needles.
TAKE TIME TO CHECK YOUR GAUGE.

STITCH GLOSSARY

RT

Pass in front of first st and k 2nd st, then k first st and let both sts fall from needle.

LT

Pass in back of first st and k 2nd st tbl, then k first st and let both sts fall from needle.

4/4 RPC

Sl 4 sts to cn and hold to back, k4, sl 1 st from cn back to LH needle, p1, k3 from cn.

4/4 LPC

Sl 4 sts to cn and hold to front, k4, sl 1 st from cn back to LH needle, p1, k3 from cn.

5/3 RPC

Sl 5 sts to cn and hold to back, k3, sl 1 st from cn back to LH needle, p1, k4 from cn.

5/3 LPC

Sl 5 sts to cn and hold to front, k3, sl 1 st from cn back to LH needle, p1, k4 from cn.

9-st LPC

Sl 6 sts to cn and hold to front, k3, sl 3 sts from cn back to LH needle, p3, k3 from cn.

11-st LPC

Sl 7 sts to cn and hold to front, k4, sl 3 sts from cn back to LH needle, p3, k4 from cn.

Cluster st

Yo, insert hook into next st and draw up a lp, yo and draw through 2 lps on hook, [yo, insert hook into same st and draw up a lp, yo and draw through 2 lps] 3 times, yo and draw through all lps on hook.

AFGHAN

Cast on 219 sts.

Beg chart pats

Row 1 (RS) *Work 36 sts chart 1, 25 sts chart 2, 36 sts chart 3*, 25 sts chart 2; rep between *'s once. Cont in pat as established until 60 rows of chart 2 have been worked 7 times, then work 6 rows more. Bind off in pat.

FINISHING

Block piece to measurements.

EDGING

With RS facing and crochet hook, work 1 rnd sc around entire afghan.
Next rnd Ch 2, work partial cluster (work between [ ]'s twice instead of 3 times) in next st, *ch 1, skip 1 st, work cluster in next st; rep from * around. Work 2 more rnds in sc. Fasten off. Block edging.

(See charts on page 136)

Patchwork Leaves

for intermediate knitters

Vibrant hues complement artful motifs in Barbara Venishnick's afghan masterpiece. Worked in intarsia, the number of squares can be changed to tailor the finished size to suit your needs. The "Patchwork Leaves" afghan first appeared in the Winter '98/'99 issue of *Family Circle Easy Knitting*.

MATERIALS

■ *Décor* by Patons®, 3½ oz/100g, each approx 210yd/192m (80% acrylic with Bounce-Back fibers® and 20% wool)
  10 balls in #1648 plum (A)
  5 balls in #1608 olive (D)
  4 balls in #1607 lt green (E)
  3 balls each in #1652 wine (B) and #1662 dk gold (C)
  1 ball in #1646 dk pink (F)
■ One size 6 (4mm) circular needle, 40"/100cm long OR SIZE TO OBTAIN GAUGE

FINISHED MEASUREMENTS

■ 61" x 75"/155cm x 190.5cm

GAUGE

19 sts and 27 rows to 4"/10cm over pat st using size 6 (4mm) circular needle. TAKE TIME TO CHECK YOUR GAUGE.

Note

Afghan is knit all in one piece, including borders, using intarsia method.

THROW

With A, cast on 296 sts. Work in garter st for 16 rows.

Beg pat

*Row 1 (RS) Work 8 sts in garter st with A, work 70 sts of Chart 1 four times, work 8 sts in garter st with A. Cont as established through chart row 46. With A, work 4 rows garter st over all sts. Work 46 rows of chart as before, but reverse squares 1 and 2 (see Chart 2 for placement). With A, work 4 rows garter st. Rep from * until 10 horizontal rows of pat squares have been completed. K 16 rows with A. Bind off purlwise.

FINISHING

Block lightly.

Chart 2

2	1	2	1	2	1	2	1
1	2	1	2	1	2	1	2
2	1	2	1	2	1	2	1
1	2	1	2	1	2	1	2
2	1	2	1	2	1	2	1
1	2	1	2	1	2	1	2
2	1	2	1	2	1	2	1
1	2	1	2	1	2	1	2
2	1	2	1	2	1	2	1
1	2	1	2	1	2	1	2

(See charts on page 137)

Windowpane Warmth

for beginner knitters

Warm apple pie, the smell of burning leaves, evenings by the fire—nothing tops off an autumn evening better than this patchwork-inspired knit afghan. The combination of warm tones and seed-stitch texture inspire cuddling on chilly nights. The "Windowpane Warmth" afghan first appeared in the Fall '97 issue of *Family Circle Easy Knitting.*

MATERIALS

■ *Sand* by Classic Elite Yarns 1¾oz/50g hanks, each approx 77yd/71m (cotton)
  20 hanks in #6416 cream
  6 hanks in #2055 red
■ *Newport* by Classic Elite 1¾oz/50g hanks, each approx 70yd/65m (cotton)
  17 hanks in #2083 orange
■ Size 7 (4.5mm) circular needdle 47"/120cm long OR SIZE TO OBTAIN GAUGE
■ Bobbins

FINISHED MEASUREMENTS

55" x 68"/140cm x 173cm

GAUGE

19 sts and 27 rows to 4"/10cm over St st with B using size 7 (4.5mm) needle.
TAKE TIME TO CHECK YOUR GAUGE.

Notes

1 Afghan is worked using circular needles back and forth as if straight needles.
2 Use separate bobbins of yarn for each section of color.
3 Twist yarns on WS to prevent holes.

STITCHES USED

Seed st
Row 1 (WS) *K1, p1; rep from *.
Row 2 (RS) *P1, k1; rep from *.
Rep rows 1 and 2 for seed st.

AFGHAN

With A, cast on 220 sts.
Rows 1-7 Work in seed st.
Next row (WS) Work seed st over 5 sts, p 210 sts, inc 15 sts evenly over these 210sts, work seed st over 5 sts—235 sts.
Next row(RS) With A, work seed st over 5 sts, beg chart row 1 rep over next 225 sts, with A; work seed st over last 5 sts. Keeping first and last 5 sts in A and seed st, work chart rows 1-28 15 times, then work rows 1-7 once.
Next row (WS) With A, work seed st over 5 sts, p 225 sts, dec 25 evenly across the 225 sts, work 5 sts in seed st—220 sts. With A, cont in seed st for 6 rows more. Bind off.

#37 Chart

Color Key

☐ With A, k on RS; p on WS
⊟ With A, p on RS; k on WS
▓ With B, k on RS; p on WS
▒ With C, k on RS; p on WS

Baby Blankets

Welcome your little one into the world with Baby's very first heirloom.

Playful Pastels

for beginner knitters

Maria Matteucci's lovingly handknit baby blanket fashions delicate seed stitch in pretty pastel shades. The diamond squares are stitched together on the diagonal creating an interesting pattern and self-finishing edge. The blanket first appeared in the Spring/Summer '01 issue of *Family Circle Easy Knitting*.

MATERIALS

■ *Windsurf* by Sesia/Lane Borgosesia, 1¾ oz/50g balls, each approx 150yd/108m (cotton)
   3 balls in #148 green (A)
   2 balls each in #203 blue (B), #89 lilac (C) and #99 yellow (D)
■ One pair size 5 (3.75mm) needles OR SIZE TO OBTAIN GAUGE

FINISHED MEASUREMENTS

■ 21" x 28"/53cm x 71cm

GAUGE

1 seed st square to 2½"/6cm over using size 5 (3.75mm) needles.
TAKE TIME TO CHECK YOUR GAUGE.

SEED STITCH

Over an even number of stitches
Row 1 (RS) *K1, p1; rep from * to end.
Row 2 *P 1, k1; rep from * to end.
Rep rows 1 and 2 for seed st.

SQUARES

Make 24 in A, 18 in D, 15 in B, 15 in C. Cast on 14 sts and work in seed st for 19 rows. Bind off.

FINISHING

With D, sew squares tog using whip st and foll placement diagram. With C, work whip st around entire outside edge of afghan, then work in other direction to form cross sts.

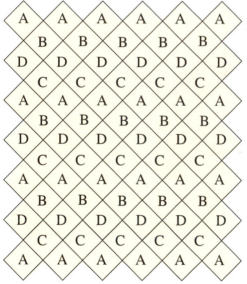

Go, Baby, Go

for intermediate knitters

Give your little one a super start with this hot set of cool wheels. Bold blocks of bright color and seed-stitch texture adorn this collection of intarsia cars and trucks, all knit in one piece, with a backward-crochet border. Designed by Michele Rose, "Go, Baby, Go" was first featured in the Fall '95 issue of *Family Circle Easy Knitting*.

MATERIALS
- *Knitusa* by Lana Borgosesia 3½ oz/100g, each approx 110yd/100m (wool)
  3 skeins each in #3793 red (A) and #25536 royal (C)
  2 skeins each in #25397 chartreuse (B), #25418 golden rod (E), #25392 fuchsia (G), #41592 light blue (F) and #nero (H)
  1 skein each #1205 ecru (J), #20266 grey (I) and #25543 purple (D)
- Size 10 (6mm) knitting needles OR SIZE NEEDED TO OBTAIN GAUGE
- Size J/10 (6mm) crochet hook
- Tapestry needle

FINISHED MEASUREMENTS
- 36" x 53"/194cm x 135cm (including crochet edging)

GAUGE
13 sts and 18 rows to 4"/10cm on size 10 (6mm) needles in St st.
TAKE TIME TO CHECK YOUR GAUGE.

Notes
1 Afghan is worked in one piece. Use a separate length of yarn for each block of color.
2 When changing yarns on same row, bring new color under old color to twist yarns to prevent holes.
3 Always work last row on each block in rev St st.

STITCHES USED
Seed Stitch
Row 1 (RS) *K1, p1; rep from * to end.
Row 2 *P1, k1; rep from * to end. Rep these 2 rows for seed st.

GARTER RIDGE
*5 rows St st, 1 row rev St st; rep from * (6 rows) for garter ridge.

AFGHAN
With size 10 (6mm) needles and A, cast on 116 sts. K 2 rows.

Beg chart
Next row (RS) K20 sts with B, k19 with C, k19A, k19D, k19E, k20C. Cont in chart pat as est, k first and last st of every row for selvage st, through chart row 52, then rep rows 1—52 three times more, work rows 1—26 once. Change to A and k 2 rows. Bind off all sts with A.

FINISHING
With tapestry needle, work 1 cross st in center of each wheel, choosing colors as desired. With A, work 1 cross st at intersection of all squares. With crochet hook and A, work 1 row of sc evenly around edge of afghan, then work 1 row of backwards sc. Fasten off.

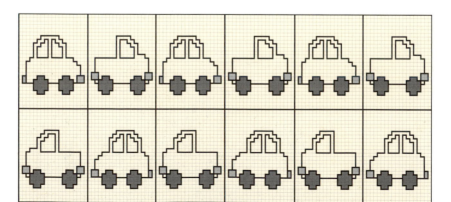

Baby Love

for intermediate knitters

Show Baby that he or she has stolen your heart by stitching it onto this delightful sampler by Michele Rose. An explosion of color, texture, and surface embroidered embellishments, this patchwork pleasure is knit all in one piece and features intarsia knitting, candy colors, and a gallery of knit and embroidery stitches. The "Baby Love" blanket was first featured in the Fall '95 issue of *Family Circle Knitting*.

MATERIALS
■ *Jiffy* by Lion Brand Yarn Co., 3oz/85g balls each approx 135yd/124m (Monsanto® acrylic)
   2 skeins each #189 sienna (A), #181 country green (B) and #101 melon (G)
   1 skein each #144 Lilac (F), #111 denim heather (E), #149 silver (J),
   #104 dusty rose (D), #157 golden rod (C), #140 rose (H) and #125 taupe (I)
■ Size 10 (6mm) knitting needles OR SIZE TO OBTAIN GAUGE
■ Size J/10 (6mm) crochet hook
■ Tapestry needle

FINISHED MEASUREMENTS
■ 37" x 45"/94cm x 114cm (including crochet edging)

GAUGE
13 sts and 19 rows to 4"/10cm on size 10 needles in St st.
TAKE TIME TO CHECK GAUGE.

Note
Afghan is worked in one piece. Use a separate length of yarn for each block of color. When changing yarns on same row, bring new color under old color and twist yarns to prevent holes.

STITCHES USED
Seed St
Ridge Pat #1
*3 rows St st, 1 row rev St st; rep from *.
Ridge Pat #2
*2 rows St st, 2 rows rev St st.

SQUARES
#1: Background: St st with B; Heart: St st with D; Embroidery: Horizontal ch st with F, vertical ch st with E, straight st with G.
#2: Background: Seed st with C; Heart: St st with E; Embroidery: French knots with G.
#3: Background: St st with D; Heart: rev St st with H; Embroidery: Cross st with J.
#4: Background: Ridge pat #1 with E; Heart: Ridge Pat #2 with A; Embroidery: Running st (over 2 rows, under 2 rows) with B.
#5: Background: Ridge Pat #1 with A; Heart: rev St st with I; Embroidery: Running st with C
#6: Background: St st with F; Heart: Seed st with G; Embroidery: Straight st with D.
#7: Background: Garter st with B; Heart: St st with J; Embroidery: French knots with A.
#8: Background: St st with G; Heart: St st with C; Embroidery: Diamonds in straight st with F, around heart straight st with E and French knots with D.
#9: Background: Garter st #1 with G; Heart: St st with J; Embroidery: Straight st with E.

#10: Background: Ridge pat #1 with H; Heart: Seed st with B; Embroidery: Chain st with F.
#11: Background: St st with C; Heart: St st with D; Embroidery: Chain st with G, Running st with B.
#12: Background: Seed st with I; Heart: St st with F; Embroidery: Straight st with J.

AFGHAN
With size 10 (6mm) needles and A, cast on 135 sts. K 2 rows.
Beg Pats—Next row (RS) K20 sts with B, k19 with C, k19D, k19E, k19D, k19C, k20B. Cont in chart pat as est, k first and last st of every row for selvage st, working individual Heart charts as described and foll placement chart on page 90. Change to A and k 2 rows. Bind off all sts with A.

FINISHING
With tapestry needle and A, work 1 cross st at intersection of all squares. With crochet hook and A, work 1 row of sc evenly around edge of afghan, then work 1 row of backwards sc (from left to right). Fasten off.

(See charts on page 138)

Her First Blanket

for intermediate knitters

Combine seed-stitched squares, gingham checks, and a host of friendly farm friends to create a blanket she'll cherish well past babyhood. Fanciful embroidered daisies and a dainty lace edging add a feminine flourish. The duplicate-stitch farm characters take the work out of colorwork. "Her First Blanket" first appeared in the Spring/Summer '98 issue of *Family Circle Easy Knitting*.

MATERIALS

- *Astra* by Patons®, 1¾oz/50g skeins, each approx 178yd/163m (acrylic)
  2 skeins in #2895 dk pink (K)
  1 skein each in #2941 yellow (A), #2902 yellow (B), #2751 white (C), #2774 lt blue (E), 2912 med green (F), #2911 lime (G), #2740 purple (H), #2724 lavender (I), #2225 red (J), #2210 med pink (L), #2901 orange (N), #2913 med brown (O), #2747 navy (P)
- 28" x 28"/71cm x 71cm square of flannel fabric for backing
- One pair each sizes 5 and 6 (3.75 and 4mm) needles OR SIZES TO OBTAIN GAUGES
- Tapestry needle

FINISHED MEASUREMENTS

- 28" x 28"/71cm x 71cm square

GAUGES

One plaid square, 31 sts and 40 rows to 5⅛"/13cm square using smaller needles.
One St st square, 31 sts and 40 rows to 5⅛"/13cm square using larger needles.
TAKE TIME TO CHECK YOUR GAUGE.

Note

When working plaid squares, carry color not in use to border sts each side to keep squares even.

AFGHAN

Plaid squares

(Make 8)

With smaller needles and dk color, cast on 31 sts. Foll chart, k1 row p1 row. Then foll chart, work rows 3-14 once, [rows 7-14] 3 times. Work rows 15 and 16 with dk color. Bind off. Make 2 squares in each of the foll 4 color combinations:

1. Dk color = br yellow (A); lt color = yellow (B); white (C).

2. Dk color = red (J); lt color = orange (N); white (C).

3. Dk color = dk pink (K), lt color = med pink (L); white (C).

4. Dk color = purple (H); lt color = lavender (I); white (C).

Stockinette st square

(Make 17)

With larger needles, and given color, cast on 31 sts. Work in St st for 40 rows. Bind off. Mark 3 squares in br yellow (A) (1 embroidered with cow); 1 square in yellow (B) sts around front neck. Work in reverse St st for 5 rows. Bind off. Work back neck in same way on 33 (35, 37, 37) sts. Embroider flowers randomly along MC section of legs using all colors in lazy daisy st with French knot centers. Centering chart 2 in A section, embroider cat in duplicate st. Embroider eyes and whiskers foll photo. Sew side seams. With smaller needles and D, pick up and k 54 (58, 62, 66) sts around armholes and work as for neckbands. Slip st all bands in place to WS. Sew 2 snap fasteners to front and back shoulders and 4 snap fasteners to leg openings with front overlapping back.

(See charts on page 139)

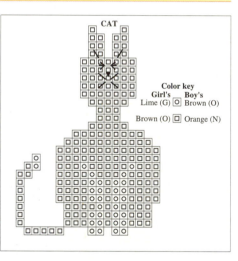

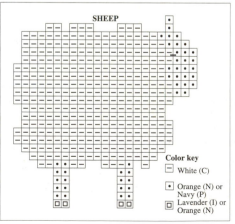

His First Blanket

for intermediate knitters

Awash in blue, this boy's blanket, features whimsical animals, bright gingham checks, and a bold striped border. Knit in squares and accented with duplicate stitch, this cuddly treasure will become a dear companion. "His First Blanket" first appeared in the Spring/Summer '98 issue of *Family Circle Easy Knitting*.

MATERIALS

- *Astra* by Patons®, 1¾ oz/50g skeins, each approx 178yd/163m (acrylic)
  2 skeins in #2747 navy (P)
  1 skein each in #2941 br yellow (A), #2902 yellow (B), #2751 white (C), #2763 med blue (D), #2774 lt blue (E), #2912 med green (F), #2911 lime (G), #2740 purple (H), #2724 lavender (I), #2895 dk pink (K), #2210 med pink (L), #2901 orange (N) and #2913 med brown (O).
- 30" x 30"/75cm x 75cm square of flannel fabric for backing
- One pair each sizes 5(3.75mm) and 6(4mm) needles OR SIZES TO OBTAIN GAUGES
- Size C/2 (2.5mm) crochet hook
- Tapestry needle

FINISHED MEASUREMENTS

- 27" x 27"/68.5cm x 68.5cm

GAUGES

One plaid square, 31 sts and 40 rows to 5"/13cm square using size 5 (3.75mm) needles.
One St st square, 31 sts and 40 rows to 5"/13cm square using size 6 (4mm) needles.
TAKE TIME TO CHECK YOUR GAUGES.

Note

1 When working plaid squares, carry color not in use to border sts each side to keep squares even.
2 See page 139 for all charts.

AFGHAN

Plaid squares

(Make 8)
With size 5 (3.75mm) needles and dk color, cast on 31 sts. Foll chart, k1 row, p1 row. Then foll chart, work rows 3-14 once, [rows 7-14] 3 times. Work rows 15 and 16 with dk color. Bind off.
Make 2 squares in each of the foll 4 color combinations:
1. Dk color = br yellow (A); lt color = yellow (B); white (C).
2. Dk color = med blue (D), lt color = lt blue (E); white (C).
3. Dk color = med green (F); lt color = lime (G); white (C).
4. Dk color = purple (H); lt color = lavender (I); white (C).

Stockinette st square

(Make 17)
With size 6 (4mm) needles and given color, cast on 31 sts. Work in St st for 40 rows. Bind off. Make 2 squares in br yellow (A) (1 embroidered with pig); 2 squares in yellow (B) (1 embroidered with horse, 1 with cat); 2 squares in med blue (D); 1 square in med green (F) (embroidered with sheep); 2 squares in lime (G) (1 embroidered with rooster, 1 with cow); 3 squares in purple (H) (1 embroidered with horse); 1 square in lavender (I) (embroidered with cow); 2 squares in navy (P) (1 embroidered with sheep, 1 with pig); 2 squares in orange (N) (1 embroidered with man, 1 with woman).

FINISHING

Block pieces lightly. Work duplicate stitch embroidery on squares foll charts. Foll alternate chart colors for horse and sheep as in photo. Embroider eyes, tails and other features in straight st, stem st and French knot as in photo. Embroider sheep with random French knots. Foll photo for square placement (including direction of squares), sew 5 rows of 5 squares each tog.

BORDER

Border is worked using colors in a random order having stripes that are 2 or 4 rows wide, as desired, in pat as foll: With size 5 (3.75mm) needles, cast on 9 sts. K2 rows, * work 5 rows in St st, k next WS row; rep from * until border fits along one side of afghan plus 1"/2.5cm to fit cast-on edge of next border. Work 3 more borders in same way. Sew borders in place around outside.

CROCHET EDGE

With crochet hook and P, sc evenly around border of afghan, working 2 sc in each corner. Join and ch 1, and work 4 more rnds of sc in each sc. Fasten off. Fold in backing fabric for ½"/1.5cm and sew to WS of afghan with thread, inside crochet edge.

Cradle Comfort

for intermediate knitters

Welcome wee ones into the world with soft texture and lovingly crafted stitch patterns. This cozy crib blanket surrounds Baby in gently twisted cables, diamonds worked in knit and purl combinations, and a richly ridged garter-stitch border. Simple to knit in one piece, this blanket, first featured in the Fall '99 issue of *Family Circle Easy Knitting,* will ensure sweet dreams for years to come.

MATERIALS

- *Astra* by Patons®, 1¾ oz/50g skeins, each approx 178yd/163m (acrylic) 7 skeins in #2783 off white
- One pair size 5 (3.75mm) needles OR SIZE TO OBTAIN GAUGE
- Cable needle

FINISHED MEASUREMENTS

- 26" x 34"/66cm x 86cm

GAUGE

23 sts and 37 rows to 4"/10cm over chart pat using size 5 (3.75mm) needles.
TAKE TIME TO CHECK YOUR GAUGE.

RIGHT CABLE PANEL

(over 9 sts, inc'd to 13)

Preparation row 1 (RS) K in front and back of next st, p in front and back of next st, k5, p in front and back of next st, k in front and back of next st.

Row 2 and all WS rows K the knit sts and p the purl sts.

Rows 3, 5, 9 and 11 K2, p2, k5, p2, k2. Row 7 K2, p2, sl 2 sts to cn and hold to back, k3, k2 from cn, p2, k2. Rep rows 2-11 for right cable panel.

LEFT CABLE PANEL

Work as for right cable panel, but work row 7 as foll: K2, p2, sl 3 sts to cn and hold to front, k2, k3 from cn, p2, k2.

Chart pat

Work all RS (odd-numbered) rows as foll: Beg with first st of chart, work to last st, skip last (center) st and work chart back from left to right to first st. P all WS rows.

AFGHAN

Cast on 147 sts and p 11 rows.

Beg pats

Next row (RS) P6, work 9 sts right cable panel, 117 sts chart pat, 9 sts left cable pat, p6—155 sts. Cont in pats as established, keeping first and last 6 sts as p every row, until 42 rows of chart pat have been worked 7 times. P next row, dec 4 sts over each cable panel—147 sts. P 9 rows more. Bind off all sts.

Stitch Key
- ☐ K on RS, p on WS
- ● P on RS, k on WS

↑Center st

Patterned Perfection

for intermediate knitters

This dazzling blanket paints Baby's world in dashing strokes of vibrant colors. A brilliant geometric pattern is repeated throughout this nursery jewel, which is knit all in one piece and finished with a wide garter-stitch border. The "Patterned Perfection" afghan first appeared in the Winter '99/'00 issue of *Family Circle Easy Knitting*.

MATERIALS

- *Micro-Spun* by Lion Brand Yarn Co., 2½oz/70g balls, each approx 240yd/216m (microfiber acrylic)
  7 (8, 8) balls in #113 red (MC)
  1 ball each in #148 turquoise (A), #194 lime (B), #158 buttercup (C), #146 fuchsia (D) and #153 black (E)
- One pair each sizes 4(3.5) and 5(3.75mm) needles OR SIZE TO OBTAIN GAUGE
- Five ¾"/19mm buttons
- Stitch holders

FINISHED MEASUREMENTS

- Chest (buttoned) 21(24¼, 27¼)"/54.5 (61.5, 69)cm
- Length 10 (11, 11½)"/25 (28, 29.5)cm
- Upper arm 10 (11, 12)"/25.5 (28, 30.5)cm

GAUGE

23 sts and 28 rows to 4"/10cm over St st using larger needles.
TAKE TIME TO CHECK YOUR GAUGE.

BLANKET

With larger needles and E, cast on 160 sts. Work rows 1-23 of chart 2. Cont with MC only for 5"/12.5cm. Work rows 1-23 of chart 2. Cont with MC only for 6"/15cm. Work rows 1-23 of chart 1. Cont with MC for 5"/12.5cm. Work rows 1-23 of chart 1. Bind off.

TOP BORDER

With RS facing, larger needles and MC, pick up and k 160 sts evenly along top of blanket. Work in garter st for 2"/5cm, inc 1 st each side every other row. Bind off.

BOTTOM BORDER

Work as for top border along bottom of blanket.

SIDE BORDERS

With RS facing, larger needles and MC, pick up and k 172 sts evenly along one side edge. work in garter st for 2"/5cm, inc 1 st each side every other row. Bind off. Work in same way along other side edge. Sew corners tog.

CARDIGAN
Body

With smaller needles and MC, cast on 119 (135, 151) sts. Work in k1, p1 rib for 1"/2.5cm, inc 1 st at end of last row—120 (136, 152) sts. Change to larger needles and work in St st as foll:

Beg chart 1

Row 1 (RS) Work 40-st rep 3 times, work first 0 (16, 32) sts once more. Cont in pat as established through chart row 23. Cont with MC only to end of piece and work even until piece measures 5 (5, 5)"/12.5 (14, 14)cm from beg, end with a WS row.

Divide for fronts and back

Next row (RS) Work 27 (31, 35) sts and place on a holder for right front, bind off 2 sts for armhole, work to end of row.

Next row (WS) Work 27 (31, 35) sts and place on a holder for left front, bind off 2 sts for armhole, work to end of row—62 (70, 78) sts for back. Work even on back sts only until armhole measures 5 (5½, 6)"/12.5 (14, 15.5)cm. Bind off all sts.

RIGHT FRONT

Sl 27 (31, 35) sts from right front holder to larger needle and cont in St st until armhole measures 3(4, 4)"/8.5 (10, 11.5)cm, end with a WS row.

NECK SHAPING

Next row (RS) Bind off 6 (7, 7) sts (neck edge), work to end. Dec 1 st at neck edge on next row, then every other row 3 times more. When same length as back, bind off rem 17 (20, 24) sts for shoulder.

LEFT FRONT

Work to correspond to right front, reversing neck shaping.

SLEEVES

With smaller needles and MC, cast on 29 (31, 33) sts. Work in k1, p1 rib for ¾"/2cm, inc 0 (1, 0) st on last row—29 (32, 33) sts. Change to larger needles and work in St st, inc 1 st each side every other row 15 (14, 11) times, then every 4th row 0 (2, 7) times—59 (64, 69) sts. Work even until piece measures 6 (7, 9)"/15.5 (17.5, 23)cm from beg. Bind off all sts.

FINISHING

Block pieces to measurements. Sew shoulder seams.

NECKBAND

With RS facing, smaller needles and MC, pick up and k 63 (67, 67) sts evenly around neck edge. Work in k1, p1 rib for ½"/1.5cm. Bind off in rib.

BUTTON BAND

With RS facing, smaller needles and MC, pick up and k 55(61, 65) sts evenly along left front edge (for girl's) or right front edge (for boy's). Work in k1, p1 rib for ½"/2cm. Bind off in rib. Place markers on band for 5 buttons, the first and last ones at ¼"/.5cm from each end and the other 3 spaced evenly between.

BUTTONHOLE BAND

Pick up sts along opposite front and work rib as before, working buttonholes in center of band opposite markers as foll: bind off 2 sts for each buttonhole. On foll row, cast on 2 sts over bound-off sts. Set in sleeves. Sew sleeve seams. Sew on buttons.

HAT
Crown

With smaller needles and MC, cast on 87 sts. Work in k1, p1 rib for 1"/2.5cm, inc 1 st at end of last row—88 sts. Change to larger needles and work in St st as foll:

Beg chart 1

Row 1 (RS) Work 40-st rep twice, work first 8 sts once more. Cont in pat as established through chart row 16, inc 1 st each side on last row—90 sts. Cont in chart pat through row 23. P 1 row with MC.

SHAPE TOP

Next row (RS) With MC, [k2tog, k8] 9 times—81 sts. P 1 row with MC. Cont in St st and stripes as foll: 4 rows A, 4 rows B, then cont with C to end of piece, AT SAME TIME, cont shaping as foll: Cont to dec 9 sts evenly every other rnd until there are 9 sts. Cut yarn, leaving an end for sewing. Draw through rem sts, pull tog tightly and secure.

FINISHING

Sew back seam. With B, make a 3"/9cm pom pom and sew to top of hat.

SOCKS

With smaller needles and MC, cast on 43 sts. Work in k1, p1 rib for ½"/1.5cm, inc 1 st on last row—44 sts. Change to larger needles. Work rows 1-8 of chart 1.

Next row (RS) *K1 D, k3 C; rep from * to end.
Next row *P2 C, p2 D; rep from * to end.
Next row K2tog and k1 with D, with C, k1, *k3 D, k1 C; rep from * to last 4 sts, k2 D, k2tog with D—42 sts.
Next row P with D, dec 1 st each side—40 sts.
Next row K with E, dec 4 sts evenly spaced across—36 sts.
Next row P with E, dec 4 sts evenly spaced across—32 sts. Cont with MC as foll:
Next row Knit.

SHAPE HEEL

Next row (WS) P9, turn. Cont in St st on these 9 sts for 9 more rows.
Next row P3, p2tog, p1, turn.
Next row Sl 1, k4.
Next row P4, p2tog, p1, turn.
Next row Sl 1, k5.
Next row P5, p2tog. Leave rem 6 sts on a holder. With WS facing, sl center 14 sts on a holder, rejoin yarn to rem 9 sts, p to end. Cont in St st on these 9 sts for 8 more rows.
Next row K3, k2tog tbl, k1, turn.
Next row Sl 1, p4.
Next row K4, k2tog tbl, k1, turn.
Next row Sl 1, p5.
Next row K5, k2tog tbl, turn.
Next row Sl 1, p5.

SHAPE INSTEP

Next row K6, pick up and k 8 sts evenly spaced along inside edge of heel, k14 from holder, pick up and k 8 sts evenly spaced along other inside edge of heel, k6 from rem holder—42 sts. P 1 row.
Next row K12, k2tog, k14, k2tog tbl, k12—40 sts. P 1 row.
Next row K11, k2tog, k14, k2tog tbl, k11—38 sts. P 1 row.
Next row K10, k2tog, k14, k2tog tbl, k10—36 sts. P 1 row.
Next row K9, k2tog, k14, k2tog tbl, k9—34 sts. Work even in St st for 15 rows more, or 1"/4cm less than desired length to toe shaping. Work 2 rows with C.

SHAPE TOE

Next row K1, *k2tog tbl, k6; rep from *, end k1. P 1 row.
Next row K1, *k2tog tbl, k5; rep from *, end k1. P 1 row.
Next row K1, *k2tog tbl, k4; rep from *, end k1. P 1 row.
Next row K1, *k2tog tbl, k3; rep from *, end k1. P 1 row.
Next row K1, *k2tog tbl, k2; rep from *, end k1. P 1 row.
Next row P2tog across. Cut yarn and draw through rem sts. Pull tog tightly and secure.

FINISHING

Sew back seam.

Color Key
+ Turquoise (A)
× Lime (B)
○ Buttercup (C)
■ Fuchsia (D)
□ Black (E)

Chart 1

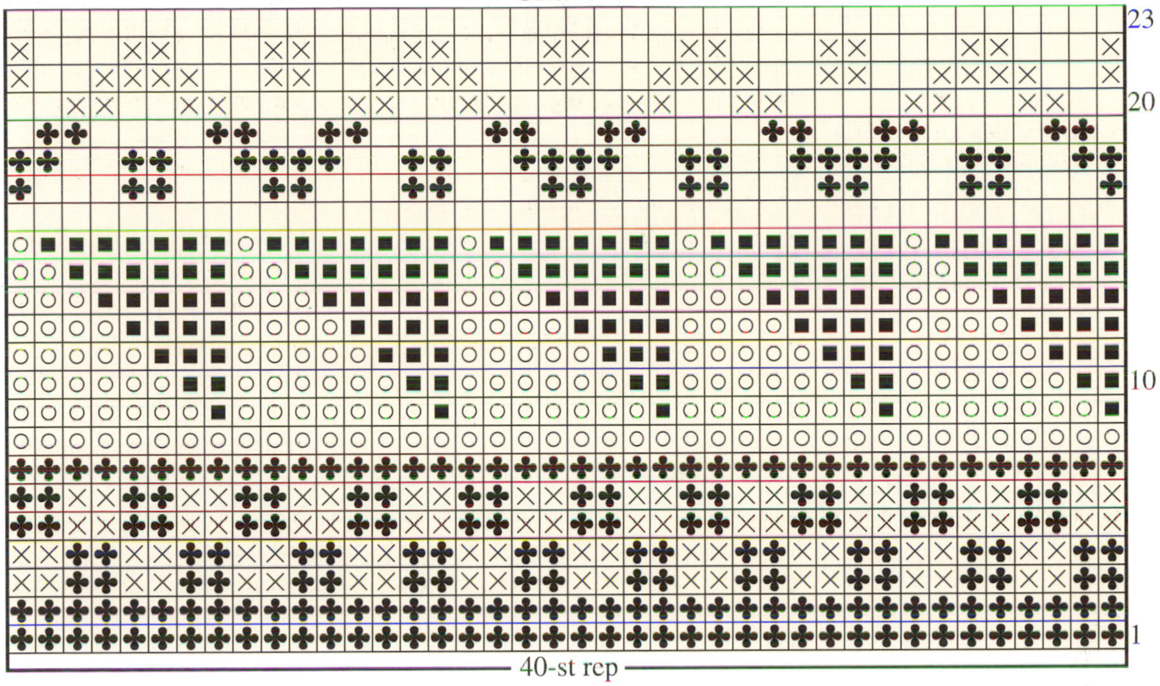

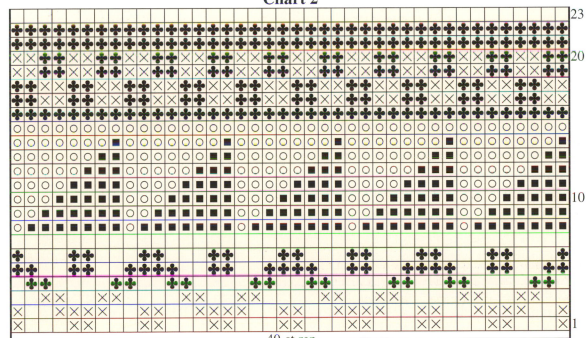

── 40-st rep ──

Chart 2

── 40-st rep ──

Little Lamb Lullaby

for intermediate knitters

Babies will love to snuggle into the curly wool of these fleecy friends, scattered across the front of Amy Bahrt's afghan. The intarsia lambs are worked into vivid stockinette squares that are stitched together and rounded up with a garter stitch border. Fleece knit in a bouclé yarn, three-dimensional ears, and french-knot eyes make these lambs spring to life. This afghan was first featured in the Fall '00 issue of *Family Circle Easy Knitting*.

MATERIALS

- *Cleckheaton Country 8-ply* by Plymouth Yarn, 1³/₄oz/50g balls, each approx 105yd/96m (wool)
  4 balls each in #0288 royal (A) and #2194 green (B)
  3 balls in #2178 red (C)
  1 ball in #2185 caramel (D)
- Wool Bouclé, 1³/₄" oz/50g balls, each approx 102yd/95m(wool)
  1 ball in #1890 white (E)
- One pair size 6 (4mm) needles OR SIZE TO OBTAIN GAUGE
- Size F/5 (4mm) crochet hook
- Bobbins (optional)

FINISHED MEASUREMENTS

- 27" x 36"/68.5cm x 91cm

GAUGE

20 sts and 26 rows to 4"/10cm over St st using size 6 (4mm) needles.
TAKE TIME TO CHECK YOUR GAUGE.

Notes

1 Blanket is worked in one piece or it may be worked in 4 separate strips and sewn tog.
2 Use a separate ball of yarn for each block of color. Use a separate ball/bobbin of B for garter st edges.
3 When changing colors, twist yarns tog on WS to prevent holes.

AFGHAN

Cast on 5 sts B, 32 sts B, 32 sts A, 32 sts C, 32 sts A, 5 sts B—138 sts. Keeping the first and last 5 sts in garter st in B, work blocks in St st foll diagram for color and chart pat (each block is 32 sts and 36 rows). Bind off.

FINISHING

Block afghan. With RS facing and B, pick up 138 sts evenly along top and bottom edge. Work in garter st for 8 rows. Bind off.

LAMB

With A, work a French knot for eyes. With crochet hook and D, ch 8. Join with sl st to first ch. Sew center tog to close ear. See chart for placement.

Color Key

- ☐ Background color (MC)
- ⌇ French knot with Royal (A)
- · Red (C)
- ☒ White (E)
- ✎ Chain st with Caramel (D)

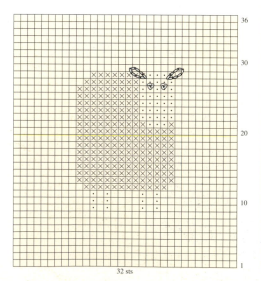

32 sts

PLACEMENT DIAGRAM

	B		
B	A	C	A
A	C	A	B
C	A	B	C
A	B	C	A
C	A	B	C
A	C	A	B
	B		

(B left and right sides)

Crochet

Fair weather comfort rendered in fresh colors, textures, and details.

Granny Squares

for beginner knitters

The old-fashioned look of granny squares is brought into the 21st century in this quick-to-crochet classic, the perfect project for a novice crocheter and a welcome gift for any home. The "Granny Squares" afghan first appeared in the Winter '99/'00 issue of *Family Circle Easy Knitting*.

MATERIALS
- *Homespun* by Lion Brand Yarn Co., 6oz/170g skeins, each approx 185yd/169m (100% Acrilan® Acrylic)
  5 skeins in #302 blue multi (A)
  2 skeins each #321 blue (B) and #309 cream (C)
- Size K/10.5 (7mm) crochet hook OR SIZES TO OBTAIN GAUGE

FINISHED MEASUREMENTS
- 45½" x 58½"/115.5cm x 148.5cm

GAUGE
1 square to 6½" x 6½"/16.5cm x 16.5cm using size K/10.5 (7mm) crochet hook.
TAKE TIME TO CHECK GAUGE.

AFGHAN
(Make 31 (32) squares)
With A (B), ch 4, join with sl st to form ring.
Rnd 1 With A (B), ch 3, 2 dc into ring, ch 1, [3 dc into ring, ch 1] 3 times; join with sl st to 3rd ch of beg ch. Fasten off.
Rnd 2 Join C (A), ch 3 (into 1-ch space from previous rnd), in same space work 2 dc, ch 1, 3 dc (first corner), [ch 1, skip 3 dc, in next space work 3 dc, ch 1, 3 dc] 3 times, ch 1; join with sl st. Fasten off.
Rnd 3 Join A (C), ch 3 (into corner space from previous rnd), in same space work 2 dc, ch 1, 3 dc (first corner), ch 1, skip 3 dc, into next space work 3 dc, [ch 1, skip 3 dc, into next space work 3 dc, ch 1, 3 dc, ch 1, skip 3, 3 dc into next space] 3 times, ch 1; join with sl st. Fasten off.
Rnd 4 Join B (A), ch 3 (into corner space from previous rnd), in same space work 2 dc, ch 1, 3 dc (first corner), [ch 1, skip 3 dc, into next space work 3 dc] twice; [ch 1, skip3 dc, into next corner space work 3 dc, ch 1, 3 dc, {ch 1, skip 3, 3 dc into next space} twice] 3 times, ch 1; join with sl st. Fasten off.

FINISHING
Alternating squares, crochet (or sew) squares tog. Block to measurements.

Checkered Bear Blanket

for intermediate knitters

Tender teddies pose among colorful checkerboards and sporty stripes on this whimsical afghan—the ideal companion for anyone who cares for bears. The single-crocheted bear motifs come alive when embellished with cross-stitched details. This cuddly treasure first appeared in the Winter '96/'97 issue of *Family Circle Easy Knitting*.

MATERIALS

■ *Canadiana* by Patons® 3½oz/100g skeins, each approx 228yd/205m
  4 balls each #143 blue (MC) and #162 olive (E)
  3 balls #149 berry (D)
  2 balls each #81 gold (C) and #152 beige (A)
  1 ball each #107 brown (B) and #109 dk brown (F)
■ Size H (5.00 mm) crochet hook OR SIZE TO OBTAIN GAUGE

FINISHED MEASUREMENT

■ 46" x 46"/117cm x 117cm

GAUGE

14 sc and 14 rows to 4"/10cm with size H hook. Each square should measure approx. 9"/23cm square
TAKE TIME TO CHECK YOUR GAUGE.

Note

When working squares A and C, do not carry colors in use across wrong side of work, but use separate balls as required. To change color, work the last st in previous color to 2 loops on hook, then draw new color through 2 loops on hook to complete st. Do not strand across rows. Use color block technique.

SQUARE A (Make 8)
Beg Square A With MC, ch 32.
Row 1 (RS) 1sc in 2nd ch from hook and each ch across — 31 sc. Ch1, turn.
Row 2 Sc in each sc —31sc. Ch 1, turn. Cont. working Square A to end of chart. Fasten off. With B, work cross st as indicated on Square A to embroider bear motif features. With F, embroider eyes and mouth.

SQUARE B
(Make 10)
With E, ch 32.

Row 1 (RS). 1sc in 2nd ch from hook and each ch across — 31 sc. Ch 1, turn. **Row 2** Sc in each sc — 31sc. Ch1, turn. Work even in sc with 5 rows E, 7 rows each in D, E, D and E. Fasten off.

SQUARE C

(Make 7)
Beg Square C With separate balls of yarn and C, ch9, with MC, ch11, with C, ch11. **Row 2** Sc in each sc — 31 sc (working in colors as established) Ch 1. Turn. Cont working Square C to end of chart. Fasten off.

FINISHING

Assemble squares as pictured.

EDGING

Join D at any corner of Afghan and work 2 rnds of sc around outer edge, working 3 sc in each corner on each rnd. Join E and work 2 rnds more. Fasten off.

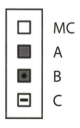

□ MC
■ A
▣ B
⊟ C

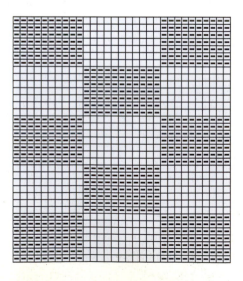

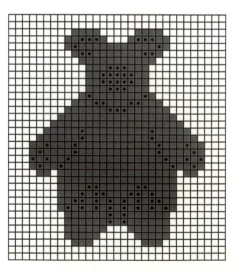

Pretty Posies

for beginner knitters

Velvety chenille in luscious, berries-and-cream colors make this bouquet of flowers absolutely irresistible. The patches of posies, worked in individual squares, are a cinch to crochet and assemble. A simple edging adds the final flourish. This spring sensation, designed by Mary Jane Protus, was first featured in the Spring/Summer '98 issue of *Family Circle Easy Knitting*.

MATERIALS

■ *Chenille Sensations* by Lion Brand Yarn Co., 1.4oz/40g balls, each approx 87yd/80m (acrylic)
  16 skeins #140 raspberry (MC)
  10 skeins #100 white (CC)
■ Size H/8 (5mm) crochet hook OR SIZE TO OBTAIN GAUGE

FINISHED MEASUREMENTS

43" x 58"/109.5cm x 147.5cm (including edging)

GAUGE

One square measures 5¼" x 5¼" (13.5cm x 13.5cm), using size H/8 (5mm) crochet hook. TAKE TIME TO CHECK YOUR GAUGE.

SQUARE

(Make 88)

With CC, ch 8, join with sl st to first ch to form ring.

Rnd 1 Ch 1, work 16 sc into ring, sl st to beg sc.

Rnd 2 Ch 2, *ch 4, sk 1 sc, 1 hdc in next sc; rep from * around, end ch 4, sl st to 3rd ch of beg ch. Fasten off.

Rnd 3 Join MC in ch-4 sp, with MC, *work in ch-4 sp (1 sc, 1 dc, 2 tr, 1 dc, 1 sc—petal made); rep from * in each ch-4 sp around, end sl st in beg sc. Fasten off.

Rnd 4 Join CC in sp between 2 sc (between 2 petals), ch 4, *[ch 5, 1 sc between 2 tr of next petal] twice, ch 5, 1 tr between next 2 sc (between petals); rep from * around, end sc in 4th ch of beg ch.

Rnd 5 Ch 3, sc in same ch as last sc of previous rnd—corner made, *ch 3, sc in ch-5 sp, ch 3, [1 sc in next sc, ch 3, 1 sc in ch-5 sp, ch 3] twice, in next tr work (1 sc, ch 3, 1 sc—corner); rep from * around, end sl st in sc at corner. Fasten off.

Rnd 6 Join MC in a corner, with MC, *work sc in corner ch-3 sp, ch 3, 1 sc in same sp, ch 3, [1 sc in ch-3 sp, ch 3] 6 times; rep from * around, end sl st in beg sc. Fasten off.

JOINING SQUARES

Horizontal rows

With MC, holding 2 squares with RS tog, work 1 sc in right corner, working into both squares, *ch 2, 1 sc in next ch-3 sp into both squares; rep from * across to next corner, ch 1, then holding 2 more squares with RS tog, work as before on these next 2 squares. Cont until there are 8 squares in one row (a total of 16 squares joined). Fasten off. Cont joining squares row by row until length is 11 squares long.

VERTICAL ROWS

Work same as Horizontal rows.

EDGE ROWS

Rnd 1 Attach MC in any corner with sc, ch 3, sc in same sp, *work 1 sc in next ch-3 sp, ch 3; rep from * around entire edge, working (1 sc, ch 3, 1 sc) in each corner, end sl st to beg sc. **Rnd 2** Sl st into corner sp, ch 1, work (1 sc, ch 3, 1 sc) in corner, work same as row 1, but ch 2 between sc worked in each ch-3 sp (except at corners). End sl st to beg sc. Fasten off.

Dazzling Diamonds

for intermediate knitters

This soft confection is as appealing to the hand as it is to the eye. Puffy popcorn stitches form diamond patterns across candy-colored squares that are worked individually, then stitched together, and topped off with a clean, double-crochet border. The "Dazzling Diamonds" afghan first appeared in the Fall '98 issue of *Family Circle Easy Knitting*.

MATERIALS

■ *Fluffy* by Unger/JCA, 1³/₄oz/50g balls, each approx 170yd/156m (acrylic)
  3 balls each in #460 white (A), #482 blue (B) and #495 lilac (C)
  2 balls each in #499 green (D) and #519 yellow (E)
■ Size G/6 (4.5mm) crochet hook OR SIZE TO OBTAIN GAUGE

FINISHED MEASUREMENTS

■ 58" x 58"/147cm x 147cm

GAUGE

One square is 8"/20.5cm using size G/6 (4.5mm) hook.
TAKE TIME TO CHECK YOUR GAUGE.

Note

Squares are made separately and sewn tog later.

STITCHES USED

Popcorn Stitch

Yo hook, insert hook into a st, draw up a lp and pull through 2 lps on hook, [yo hook, insert hook into same st, draw up a lp and pull through 2 lps on hool] 3 times, yo hook and pull through all 5 lps on hook.

Basic Square

Ch 9, join with sl st to first ch to form ring.
Rnd 1 Ch 3 (counts as 1 dc), in ring work 1 popcorn st, 1 dc, ch 3 (corner), [1 dc, 1 popcorn, 1 dc, ch 3 (corner)] 3 times, join with sl st to top of beg ch-3.
Rnd 2 Ch 4 (counts as 1 dc and ch 1) [in next corner work 1 dc, 1 popcorn, 1 dc, ch 3, 1 dc, 1 popcorn, 1 dc, ch 1] 4 times, dc in 3rd ch of ebg ch-4.
Rnd 3 Ch 4, 1 dc in next dc, ch 1, *in corner work 1 dc, 1 popcorn, 1 dc, ch 3, 1 dc, 1 popcorn, 1 dc, [ch 1, dc in next dc] twice, ch 1; rep from * around, join with sl st to 3rd ch of beg ch-4.
Rnd 4 Ch 4, *dc in next dc, ch 1] twice, work corner same as in rnd 3, [ch 1, dc in next dc] twice; rep from * around, join with sl st to 3rd ch of beg ch-4.
Rnds 5 and 6 Work same as rnd 4, working 2 more dc, ch 1 between each corner on each rnd. Fasten off.

THROW

Make 49 squares in foll colors: 13 A, 9 B, 10 C, 7 D and 10 E. Sew squares tog foll placement diagram.

FINISHING

With RS facing and B, work 2 rnds dc around outisde edge of afghan, working ch 5 in each corner on first rnd and 5 dc in each corner ch-5 on 2nd rnd, then work 1 rnd sc, working 3 sc in each corner.

Placement Diagram

B	C	D	E	B	E	C
C	B	A	C	A	D	A
A	C	E	D	E	A	D
E	B	C	E	A	C	A
D	E	B	A	B	E	C
E	A	E	B	C	D	A
A	B	C	A	D	A	B

- A White
- B Blue
- C Lilac
- D Green
- E Yellow

Cozy Cover-Up
for intermediate knitters

Granny squares take a chic turn when cast in turquoise, emerald, ruby, and garnet tones. The tiny pieces, easy to crochet on the run, are whip-stitched together with contrasting yarn to create a unique design and diamond-shaped edging. This heirloom-to-be was first featured in the Winter '98/'99 issue of *Family Circle Easy Knitting*.

MATERIALS

- *Wintuk* by Caron International, 3½oz/100g skeins, each approx 213yd/196m (100% Acrylic with Bounce-Back fibers®)
  7 skeins in #3021 oatmeal (MC)
  2 skeins each in #3032 rosewine (A), #3160 dk Colonial blue (B), #3239 teal (C), #3194 dk sage (D) and #3048 crimson (E)
- Size F/5 (4mm) crochet hook OR SIZE TO OBTAIN GAUGE

FINISHED MEASUREMENTS

- 44" x 60"/112cm x 152.5cm

GAUGE

1 granny square equals 2¼"/5.5cm square using size F/5 (4mm) crochet hook.
TAKE TIME TO CHECK YOUR GAUGE.

GRANNY SQUARE

With size F/5 (4mm) crochet hook and MC, ch 6, join with sl st to first ch to form ring.
Rnd 1 Ch 3 (counts as 1 dc), 3 dc in ring, ch 2, [4dc in ring, ch 2] 3 times, join with sl st to beg ch. Fasten off.
Rnd 2 Join CC to any ch-2 sp. Ch 3, in same sp (3 dc, ch 2, 4 dc), ch 1, [in next ch-2 sp work (4 dc, ch 2, 4 dc, ch1)] 3 times, join with sl st to beg ch. Fasten off.

THROW

Make granny squares as foll:
98 squares using A as CC.
98 squares using B as CC.
96 squares using C as CC.
92 squares using D as CC.
88 squares using E as CC.

FINISHING

With RS facing and MC, whipstitch squares tog foll placement diagram. With MC, work sc evenly around outside edge.

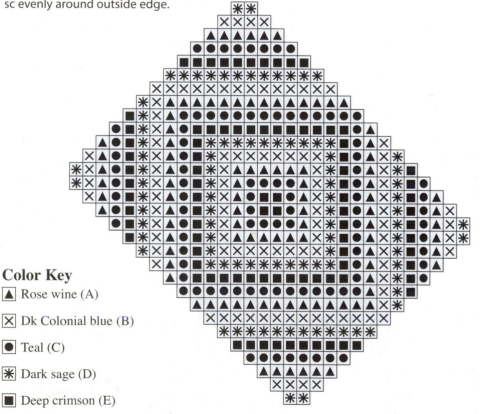

Color Key

- ▲ Rose wine (A)
- ☒ Dk Colonial blue (B)
- ● Teal (C)
- ✳ Dark sage (D)
- ■ Deep crimson (E)

Retro Chic

for intermediate knitters

Classic turns cool when an age-old granny square pattern is reinterpreted in today's funkiest colors. What remains the same is the ease with which this tradition can be created. Why not pass the technique—as well as the afghan—along to a new generation of crocheters? The "Retro Chic" afghan, designed by Maria Matteucci, first appeared in the Fall '99 issue of *Family Circle Easy Knitting*.

MATERIALS

- *Red Heart®TLC* by Coats & Clark, 5oz/140g skeins, each approx 253yd/ 233m acrylic)
  4 skeins in #5657 kiwi (MC)
- Red Heart® Soft by Coats & Clark, 5oz/140g skeins, each approx
  328yd/302m (acrylic)
  2 skeins in #7821 med blue (A)
  1 skein each in #7322 gold (B), #7815 lt blue (C), #7775 dk rose (D), #7722 lt pink (E), #7664 blue green (F) and #7773 med pink (G)
- Size H/8 (5mm) crochet hook OR SIZE TO OBTAIN GAUGE

FINISHED MEASUREMENTS

- 49" x 56"/125cm x 142cm

GAUGE

One basic square to 7½"/19cm using size H/8 (5mm) hook.
TAKE TIME TO CHECK YOUR GAUGE.

BASIC SQUARE

(Make 8 basic squares in each of the 7 variations given below—56 basic squares.)
With same color used for rnd 1, ch 4. Join with sl st to first ch to form ring.

Rnd 1 Ch 3 (counts as 1 dc), work 2 dc in ring, [ch 2, work 3 dc in ring] 3 times, ch 2. Join with sl st to top of beg ch-3. Fasten off, join 2nd color.

Rnd 2 Ch 3, in next ch-2 sp work (2 dc, ch 2, 3 dc) for first corner, ch 1, [in next ch-2 sp work (3 dc, ch 2, 3 dc), ch 1] 3 times. Join with sl st to top of beg ch-3. Fasten off, join 3rd color.

Rnd 3 Ch 3, in next ch-2 sp work (2 dc, ch 2, 3 dc) for first corner, [ch 1, work 3 dc in next ch-1 sp, ch 1, in next ch-2 sp work (3 dc, ch 2, 3 dc)] 3 times, ch 1, work 3 dc in last ch-1 sp, ch 1. Join with sl st to top of beg ch-3. Fasten off, join 4th color.

Rnd 4 Ch 3, in next ch-2 sp work (2 dc, ch 2, 3 dc) for first corner, [ch 1, work 3 dc in next ch-1 sp, ch 1, work 3 dc in next ch-1 sp, ch 1, in next ch-2 sp work (3 dc, ch 2, 3 dc)] 3 times, ch 1, work 3 dc in next ch-1 sp, ch 1, work 3 dc in last ch-1 sp, ch 1. Join with sl st to top of beg ch-3. Fasten off, join 5th color.

Rnd 5 Ch 3, in next ch-2 sp work (2 dc, ch 2, 3 dc) for first corner, [ch 1, work 3 dc, ch 1, in each of next 3 ch-1 sp, in next ch-2 sp work (3 dc, ch 2, 3 dc)] 3 times, ch 1, work 3 dc, ch 1, in each of last 3 ch-1 sp. Join with sl st to top of beg ch-3. Fasten off, join 6th color.

Rnd 6 Ch 3, in next ch-2 sp work (2 dc, ch 2, 3 dc) for first corner, [ch 1, work 3 dc, ch 1, in each of next 4 ch-1 sp, in next ch-2 sp work (3 dc, ch 2, 3 dc)] 3 times, ch 1, work 3 dc, ch 1 in each of last 4 ch-1 sp, ch 1. Join with sl st to top of beg ch-3. Fasten off, join 7th color.

Rnd 7 Ch 3, in next ch-2 sp work (2 dc, ch 2, 3 dc) for first corner, [ch 1, work 3 dc, ch 1 in each of next 5 ch-1 sp, in next ch-2 sp work (3 dc, ch 2, 3 dc)] 3 times, ch 1, work 3 dc, ch 1 in each of last 5 ch-1 sp, ch 1. Join with sl st to top of beg ch-3. Fasten off.

Square 1
1 rnd each: B, C, D, F, G, A, MC.

Square 2
1 rnd each: E, C, G, A, D, B, MC.

Square 3
1 rnd each: A, B, F, D, E, C, MC.

Square 4
1 rnd each: C, G, A, E, F, D, MC.

Square 5
1 rnd each: D, F, B, A, G, C, MC.

Square 6
1 rnd each: G, C, D, A, B, F, MC.

Square 7
1 rnd each: F, D, C, G, A, E, MC.

FINISHING

With RS facing and MC, whip stitch square tog foll placement diagram. With MC and crochet hook, work 2 rnds sc around outside edge of afghan, working 2 sc, ch 2, 2 sc in each corner ch.

Placement Diagram

1	3	2	7	6	5	4
7	6	5	4	3	2	1
1	3	2	7	6	5	4
7	6	5	4	3	2	1
1	3	2	7	6	5	4
7	6	5	4	3	2	1
1	3	2	7	6	5	4
7	6	5	4	3	2	1

Nature's Bounty

for intermediate knitters

The beauty of a trailing grapevine is captured with striking authenticity in this design. Grape-leaf motifs are cross-stitched onto panels of Tunisian crochet, then embellished with embroidered vines and crocheted-bobble grapes. An intricate chain-and-bobble edging adds the crowning touch to this glorious harvest. Nicky Epstein's "Nature's Bounty" afghan first appeared in the Winter '98/'99 issue of *Family Circle Easy Knitting*.

MATERIALS

- *Berella '4'* by Bernat®, 3½ oz/100g skeins, each approx 240yd/219m (100% acrylic with Bounce-Back fiber®)
  12 skeins in #8887 yellow (MC)
  5 skeins each in #8880 pale olive (A) and #8882 med olive (B)
  2 skeins each in #8883 olive (C) and #8799 lt eggplant (D)
  1 skein each in #8796 oak (E), #8916 walnut (F), #8817 dk rose (G), #8801 deep eggplant (H), #8804 periwinkle (I)
- Size H/8 (5mm) crochet hook OR SIZE TO OBTAIN GAUGE

FIINISHED MEASUREMENTS

- 50" x 68"/127cm x 172.5cm (excluding fringe)

GAUGE

18 sts and 16 rows to 4"/10cm over Tunisian crochet with MC using size H/8 (5mm) hook. TAKE TIME TO CHECK YOUR GAUGE.

STITCHES USED

Tunisian Crochet

Foundation row Draw up a lp in 2nd ch from hook; keeping all lps on hook, draw up a lp in each ch to end.

Row 1 Yo and draw through first lp, *yo and draw through 2 lps; rep from * until 1 lp rem on hook, this lp counts as first st of next row.

Row 2 Keeping all lps on hook, insert hook under 2nd vertical bar from hook and draw up a lp; draw up a lp under each vertical bar to last bar; insert hook under 2 strands of last st and draw up a lp. Rep rows 1 and 2 for Tunisian crochet.

AFGHAN

Grape panels

(Make 3)

With size H/8 (5mm) hook and MC, ch 54.

Work Tunisian crochet foundation row, then rep rows 1 and 2 for a total of 249 rows. Fasten off. Foll chart, work cross stitch on panels as foll: Bring tapestry needle to RS just below horizontal bar of st; pull yarn through; bring needle over vertical bar, then from top to bottom behind horizontal bar of next st. Cont across row to form first half of cross st. Work back across row, bringing needle behind crossbars as before to complete cross st. Split strand of E in half to work corkscrew vines in stem st foll chart for placement.

Grapes

(Make approx 192 with D; 90 with H; 54 with G; 27 with I and 24 with A)

With end of yarn in palm of left hand, wrap yarn around index finger, insert hook into lp around finger from underneath and draw up a lp, slip lp from finger and hold between finger and thumb of left hand *insert hook into ring and draw up a lp, yo and through 2 lps on hook; rep from * 13 times more. Cut yarn, leaving a long end. Pull end through rem st. Turn grape to RS, pull both yarn ends tightly and knot. Foll photo, and having lighter color grapes to the left side of each cluster, sew grapes to afghan.

Leaf panels

(Make 4)

With size H/8 (5mm) hook and A, ch 9. Work Tunisian crochet foundation row—9 sts, then rep rows 1 and 2 twice, row 1 once.

Row 7 With A, draw up a lp in each of next 4 vertical bars, mark last lp for center st and drop this lp from hook—4 lps on hook; with B, make a sl knot on hook, yo and draw up a long lp under 2nd vertical bar to right of center st 3 rows below, yo and through 1 lp [yo and through 2 lps] twice—4 A lps and 1 B lp on hook; yo and draw up a long lp under first vertical bar to right of center st 4 rows below, *yo and through 1 lp, yo and through 2 lps, yo and through 1 lp*—4 A lps and 2 B lps on hook; yo twice and draw up a long lp through center st 5 rows below, yo and through 1 lp [yo and through 2 lps] twice, yo and through 1 lp—4 A lps and 3 B lps on hook; yo and draw up a long lp under first vertical bar to left of center st in 4th row below, rep between *'s once—4 A lps and 4 B lps on hook; yo and draw up a long lp under 2nd vertical bar to left of center st in 3rd row below, yo and through 1 lp, yo and through 2 lps, yo and through 1 lp—4 A lps and 5 B lps on hook; yo and through 5 B

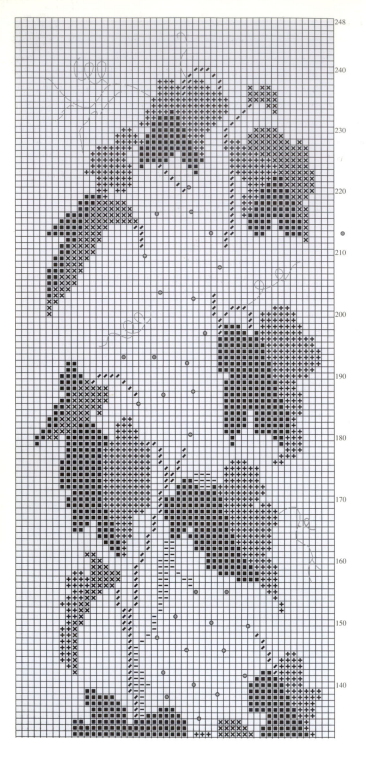

Color Key

- ■ Pale olive (A)
- + Med. olive (B)
- ✕ Olive (C)
- ◉ Bobble
- ✎ Oak (E)
- — Walnut (F)

lps—1 B leaf completed. Fasten off, leaving a long tail, draw tail through last B lp on hook and pull tightly—5 A lps on hook. Sl A center st back to hook. With A, draw up a lp under each vertical bar to last bar—9 lps on hook. Work back as for row 1 of Tunisian crochet.

Row 8 With A, rep row 2 of Tunisian crochet, working over B end to secure. Cont in Tunisian crochet with A as established, AT SAME TIME, rep row 7 every 7th row, until 35 leaves have been completed, end with a row 8. Sl st in each st across. Fasten off.

EDGING

Make two 50"/127cm lengths as foll:

Braid

With size H/8 (5mm) hook and B, ch 163.

Row 1 Sc in 2nd ch from hook and in each ch to end—162 sts.

Row 2 Ch 1 (counts as first sc), turn. Sc in each st across.

Row 3 Ch 4 (counts as first dc and ch 1), turn. *[Yo and insert hook into st, yo and draw up a lp, yo and through 2 lps on hook] in same st 9 times, yo and through all 10 lps on hook—bobble made; ch 1 tightly to secure bobble, ch 1, sk next st, dc in next st, ch 1, sk next st; rep from *, end with dc in last st.

Row 4 Ch 1 (counts as first sc), turn. *Sc in ch-sp, sc in top of next bobble, sc in next ch-sp, sc in next dc; rep from * to end.

Row 5 Ch 1, turn. Sc in each st across. Fasten off.

GRAPES FOR EDGING

With end of yarn in palm of left hand, wrap yarn around index finger, insert hook into lp around finger from underneath, yo and draw up a lp, slip lp from finger and hold between finger and thumb of left hand, *insert hook into ring, yo and draw up a lp, yo and through 2 lps on hook; rep from * 19 times more. Do not fasten off. Tighten ring by pulling beg tail of yarn. Ch 9, sl st to braid below bobble, sl st back along ch to grape, ch 9, skip next bobble, sl st to braid below next bobble, sl st back along ch and fasten to grape. Cont in this way, fastening each new grape below the bobble omitted in the previous joining, thus forming a crossover design.

FINISHING

Sew leaf panels between grape panels and to each long side of afghan. Sew edging to top and bottom of afghan.

Crochet Classic

for intermediate knitters

Small squares crocheted in delicious berry hues form a classic step pattern when assembled into Sharon Valiant's deceptively simple afghan. The motifs are crocheted onto each other to form the body of the blanket; the remaining pieces are stitched separately and then joined. A picot border is the icing on the cake. The "Crochet Classic" afghan was first featured in the Fall '99 issue of *Family Circle Easy Knitting*.

MATERIALS

■ *Homespun* by Lion Brand Yarn Co., 6oz/170g skeins, each approx 185yd/169m (acrylic)
   3 skeins in #307 berry (A)
   4 skeins in #314 purple (B)
   5 skeins in #300 white (C)
■ Size K/10 (7mm) crochet hook OR SIZE TO OBTAIN GAUGE

FINISHED MEASUREMENTS

■ 60"x 60"/152cm x 152cm

GAUGE

1 square to $4\frac{1}{2}$"/11.5cm
TAKE TIME TO CHECK YOUR GAUGE.

Note

When beg a new color, make sl knot 12"/30.5cm from end of yarn; when completing any color, cut yarn leaving 12"/30.5cm end. These ends will later be used to sew squares together.

SMALL SQUARE (Make 100)

Row 1 With A, ch 6. Dc in 4th ch from hook and in each ch to end—1 motif completed. Turn.
Row 2 Ch 6, dc in 4th ch from hook and in each ch to end, sl st in top of ch-3 of first motif, (ch 3, 3 dc over same ch-3)—2 motifs completed; motifs form a step pattern. Turn.
Row 3 Ch 6, dc in 4th ch from hook and in each ch to end, [sl st in top of next ch-3, ch 3, 3 dc over same ch-3] twice—3 motifs completed. Cut yarn leaving 12"/30.5cm end. Turn.

Row 4 (RS) Join C in top of last dc, ch 6, dc in 4th ch from hook and in each ch to end, [sl st in top of next ch-3, ch 3, 3 dc over same ch-3] 3 times—4 motifs. Cut yarn, turn.
Row 5 (dec row) Skip 3 dc, join B in top of ch-3, [ch 3, 3 dc over same ch-3, sl st in top of next ch-3] 3 times—3 motifs. Turn.
Row 6 (dec row) Sl st in 3 dc and in ch-3, [ch 3, 3 dc over same ch-3, sl st in top of next ch-3] twice—2 motifs. Turn.
Row 7 (dec row) Sl st in 3 dc and in ch-3, ch 3, 3 dc over same ch-3, sl st in top of next ch-3. Fasten off.

FINISHING

Large squares (Make 25)

Each large square requires 4 small squares. With color A triangle positioned at center, arrange 4 small squares into 2 by 2 block; take care that Row 4 is on right side of work. Working on WS, using 12"/30.5cm ends in matching colors, sew squares tog between motifs.

Assembling large squares

Using 12"/30.5cm yarn ends and working as before, sew large squares tog into 5 by 5 unit.

BORDER

Rnd 1 With RS facing, join C in corner, *3 sc in corner, (ch 2, sc between next 2 motifs) to next corner, ch 2; rep from * around, join with sl st to first sc.
Rnd 2 Ch 3 for first dc, *in center sc of corner work 2 dc, ch 2, and 2 dc, dc in next sc, (3 dc in next ch-2) to next corner**, dc in sc; rep from * around, end last rep at **, join with sl st to top of starting ch-3.
Rnd 3 Sl st to ch-2 corner, *3 sc in corner, (ch 2, skip 3 dc, sc between dc-groups) to next corner, ch 2; rep from * around, join.
Rnd 4 Rep rnd 2. Cut yarn.
Rnd 5 Join B in corner, rep rnd 3.
Rnds 6 and 7 With B, rep rnds 2 and 3. At end of last rnd, cut yarn.
Rnd 8 Join C in first sc of corner, rep rnd 2.
Rnd 9 With B, rep rnd 3.
Rnd 10 Sc in same st as joining, *in corner work sc, ch 3, sl st in last sc for picot, sc in same corner, sc in next sc, (in next ch-3 work sc, picot, sc) to corner**, sc in sc before corner; rep from * around. Join and fasten off.

Spice-Toned Treasure

for intermediate knitters

Sweet motifs in eye-catching colors make this afghan a crown jewel. Sharon Valiant's blending of a simple stitch pattern, two strands of yarn, and whip-stitch assembly guarantee that this handmade treasure will be as quick to complete as it is pleasing to behold. The "Spice-Toned Treasure" first appeared in the Winter '99/'00 issue of *Family Circle Easy Knitting*.

MATERIALS
- *Red Heart® Soft* by Coats & Clark, 5oz/140g skein, each approx 253yd/233m (100% Acrylic with Bounce Back® fibers)
  2 skeins each in #7587 purple, #7675 green, #7322 gold, #7760 cranberry, #7285 rust and #7368 brown
  1 skein in #7012 black
- Size N/15 (10mm) crochet hook OR SIZE TO OBTAIN GAUGE

FINISHED MEASUREMENTS
- 47" x 66"/119.5cm x 167.5cm

GAUGE
One square measures 4¼" x 4¼"/12cm x 12cm using size N/15 (10mm) crochet hook. TAKE TIME TO CHECK YOUR GAUGE.

Note
Work with 2 strands of yarn held tog throughout.

SQUARE
Make 140 squares in colors desired as foll:
Ch 6 and join with sl st to form a ring.
Rnd 1 Ch 5 for first dc and ch 2, [3 dc in ring, ch 2 for corner] 3 times, 2 dc in ring, join with sl st to 3rd ch of starting ch-5.
Rnd 2 Sl st in next ch-2, ch 3 for first dc, in same ch-2 work 2 dc, ch 2 and 3 dc for corner ch 1, [in next ch-2 work 3 dc, ch 2, and 3 dc for corner, ch 1] 3 times, join with sl st to top of starting ch-3. Fasten off.

FINISHING
Arrange colors randomly 10 squares by 14 squares. With 2 strands of black and tapestry needle, whip st squares tog as foll: work whip st into all cornes and ch-1 sp and into center st of each 3-dc group. When all squares are joined, work whip st around outside edge.

Chenille Dazzler

for intermediate knitters

Petal-soft colors paired with a precocious zig-zag make this cover-up equal parts sugar and spice. Melissa Leapman's modern take on the traditional ripple afghan works in a rich chenille yarn with basic double-crochet stitches that even a novice can master. The "Chenille Dazzler" afghan first appeared in the Fall '99 issue of *Family Circle Easy Knitting*.

MATERIALS

■ *Cotton Chenille* by Crystal Palace Yarns, 1¾oz/ 50g balls, each approx 98yd/89m (cotton)

  13 balls in #1404 lavender (A)

  4 balls each in #1109 pink (B) and #1058 white (C)

■ Size H/8 (5mm) crochet hook

FINISHED MEASUREMENTS

■ 38" x 50"/96.5cm x 127cm

GAUGE

1 ripple (or 1 rep) and 6 rows to 4"/10cm over ripple pat using size H/8 (5mm) crochet hook TAKE TIME TO CHECK YOUR GAUGE.

RIPPLE PAT

Ch a multiple of 24 sts plus 5.
Foundation row Dc into 5th ch from hook, *[skip next ch, 2 dc in next ch] 4 times, skip next ch, yo, insert hook into next ch and pull up a lp, yo and draw through 2 lps, skip next 3 ch, yo, insert hook into next ch and pull up a lp, yo and draw through 2 lps, yo and draw through all 3 lps (foundation dec made), [skip next ch, 2 dc in next ch] 4 times, skip next ch, [dc, ch 3, dc] in next ch; rep from *, end skip next ch, [dc, ch 1, dc] in last ch. Ch 4, turn.
Row 1 Dc in first dc, 2 dc in next ch-1 sp, *[skip next dc, 2 dc between next 2 dc] 3 times, work dec as in foundation rows (working into dc instead of ch), [skip next dc, 2 dc between next 2 dc] 3 times, [3 dc, ch 3, 3 dc] into next ch-3 sp; rep from *, end skip next dc, [3 dc, ch 1, dc] in last ch. Ch 4, turn.
Rep row 1 for ripple pat.

STRIPE PATTERN

*2 rows A, 1 row B, 2 rows A, 1 row C; rep from * (6 rows) for stripe pat.

AFGHAN

With A, ch 245. Work in ripple and stripe pats until 6 rows of stripe pat have been worked 12 times, then work 2 rows more with A. Piece measures approx 50"/96.5cm. Fasten off.

Artisan Afghan

for intermediate knitters

It's a small world after all—North African-inspired art finds its way into your own living room with this exotic afghan. Featuring a two-toned diamond design, simple single crochet, and desert-sunset colors, it will lend a touch of culture to any home. Melissa Leapman's creation first appeared in the Fall '00 issue of *Family Circle Easy Knitting*.

MATERIALS

■ *Red Heart* ® Soft by Coats & Clark, 5oz/140g balls, each approx 328yd/302m (acrylic)
  9 skeins each in #7744 dk blush (A) and #7760 cranberry (B)
■ Size H/8 (5mm) crochet hook OR SIZE TO OBTAIN GAUGE

FINISHED MEASUREMENTS

■ 46" x 69"/117cm x 175cm

GAUGE

19 sc and 20 rows to 4"/10cm using size H/8 (5mm) crochet hook.
TAKE TIME TO CHECK YOUR GAUGE.

SC PATTERN

Ch desired number.
Row 1 (RS) Sc in 2nd ch from hook and in each ch to end. Ch 1, turn.
Row 2 Sc in each sc. Ch 1, turn.
Rep row 2 for sc pat.

AFGHAN

With A, ch 214. Work in sc pat and chart pat over 213 sts as foll: Work 30-st rep 7 times, work last 3 sts of chart. Cont in pat as established until 24 rows of chart have been worked 14 times, then work rows 1-3 once more. Piece should measure approx 68"/172cm from beg. Fasten off.

FINISHING

With RS facing, attach A with a sl st to a corner and ch 1. Work 3 rnds of sc evenly around afghan, working 3 sc into each corner. Fasten off.

30-st rep

Color Key
□ Dk blush (A)
· Cranberry (B)

Aztec Traditions

for intermediate knitters

Hot and cool tones mirror the extremes of the desert in this plush, colorful afghan inspired by Navajo blankets. Finished with a striped border, the afghan is quick to crochet in a thick, terry-like yarn and half-double crochet stitches. The "Aztec Traditions" afghan first appeared in the Fall '00 issue of *Family Circle Easy Knitting*.

MATERIALS

■ *Terryspun* by Lion Brand Yarn Co., 120yd/109m balls (acrylic)
  3 balls each in #123 seaspray (A), #135 cinnamon (B) and #124 oatmeal (C)
■ Size N/15 (10mm) crochet hook OR SIZE TO OBTAIN GAUGE

FINISHED MEASUREMENTS

■ 38$\frac{1}{2}$" x 62$\frac{1}{2}$"/98cm x 159cm

GAUGE

8 hdc and 5 rows to 4"/10cm using size N/15 (10mm) crochet hook.
TAKE TIME TO CHECK YOUR GAUGE.

AFGHAN

With A, ch 68.
Beg chart
Row 1 (RS) Using chart for color changes, hdc in 3rd ch from hook and in ch to end—67 hdc (including t-ch). Ch 2, turn.
Row 2 Work in hdc, changing colors foll chart through row 72. Fasten off.

BORDER

Work 1 row sc on each side, matching colors. Beg at corner, join C with sl st in corner and work 1 rnd sc, working 3 sc in each corner. Cont in rnds of sc as foll: 1 rnd A, 1 rnd C, 1 rnd B, 1 rnd C, 1 rnd A. Fasten off.

Color Key

☐ Seaspray (A)
☒ Cinnamon (B)
⊡ Oatmeal (C)

67sts

Global Warming

for intermediate knitters

Enjoy the flavor of the East in Melissa Leapman's striking North African afghan. Three panels of bold motifs are crocheted separately in lush mohair, then whip-stitched together and finished with a spare border to create a sensuous throw. The "Global Warming" afghan first appeared in the Fall '00 issue of *Family Circle Easy Knitting*.

MATERIALS

- La Gran by Classic Elite Yarns, 1½ oz/42g, each approx 90yd/82m (mohair/wool/nylon)
  19 balls in #6533 brick (MC)
  4 balls each in #6512 green (A) and #6572 lime (B)
  2 balls each in #6585 orange (C) and #6562 blue (D)
- Size J/10 (6mm) crochet hook or SIZE TO OBTAIN GAUGE

FINISHED MEASUREMENTS

- 45" x 62"/114cm x 157.5cm

GAUGE

15 sc and 16 rows to 4"/10cm using size J/10 (6mm) crochet hook.
TAKE TIME TO CHECK YOUR GAUGE.

PANEL A

(Make 2)

With MC, ch 55. Row 1 SC into 2nd ch from hook and into each ch to end—54 sc. Ch 1, turn.

Beg Chart

Beg with row 2 and work through row 120, then work rows 1-120 once more, then rows 1 and 2 once. Fasten off.

PANEL B

(Make 1)

With MC, ch 55. Row 1 Sc into 2nd ch from hook and into each ch across—54 sc. Ch 1, turn.

Beg chart

Beg with row 62, work through row 120, then work rows 1-120 once more, then rows 1-62 once. Fasten off.

FINISHING

With RS facing and MC, whipstitch panels tog, with panel B in center.

Border

With RS facing and MC, work 2 rnds of sc evenly around afghan, working 3 sc into each corner. Work 2 rnds A, 1 rnd MC. Fasten off.

Color Key

☐ Brick (MC)
☒ Green (A)
✳ Lime (B)
⊡ Orange (C)
⊟ Blue (D)

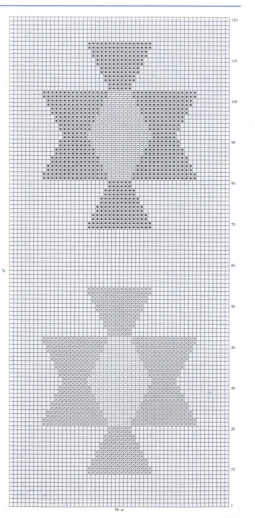

Navajo Throw

for intermediate knitters

Native American motifs are interpreted in soft neutrals in Gayle Bunn's tribute to American heritage. Here, a variation on the single crochet stitch creates a woven look while the use of long loops adds texture and incorporates color. The edging is a simple, single crochet worked once forward, then backward. The "Navajo Throw" first appeared in the Winter '98/'99 issue of *Family Circle Easy Knitting*.

MATERIALS

■ *Décor* by Patons®, 3½ oz/100g balls, each approx 210yd/192m (80% acrylic with Bounce-Back fibers® and 20% wool)
7 balls in #1630 beige (MC)
3 balls in #1632 lt brown (A)
2 balls in #1633 dk brown (B)
■ Sizes H/8 (5mm) and J/10 (6mm) crochet hooks OR SIZE TO OBTAIN GAUGE

KNITTED MEASUREMENTS
44" x 53"/111.5cm x 134cm

GAUGE
15 sts and 17 rows to 4"/10cm over woven sc pat with MC using larger hook.
TAKE TIME TO CHECK YOUR GAUGE.

STITCHES USED

Woven Single Crochet Pattern
Foundation row (WS) Sc in 2nd ch from hook, *ch 1, skip next ch, sc in next ch; rep from * to end.

Notes
1 Each ch-1 sp counts as 1 sc. Ch 1, turn.
2 When working from charts, work in sc only and carry color not in use across top of last row and work around it with new color. To change color, work to last 2 lps on hook with old color, yo and through 2 lps with new color to complete st.
Row 1 Sc in first sc, *sc in next ch-1 sp, ch 1, skip next sc; rep from * to last 2 sts, sc in next ch-1 sp, sc in last sc. Ch 1, turn.
Row 2 Sc in first sc, *ch 1, skip next sc, sc in next ch-1 sp; rep from * to end. Ch 1, turn. Rep last 2 rows for woven sc pat.

THROW
With smaller hook and MC, ch 168. Change to larger hook. Work foundation row of woven sc pat—167 sts. Rep row 1 and 2 of woven sc pat twice. **Change to smaller hook and sc.

Beg Chart 1
Work 8-st rep 20 times, then work first 7 sts once more. Cont as established through chart row 7. Change to larger hook and MC.
Next row (WS) Sc in first sc, *ch 1, skip next sc, sc in next sc; rep from * to end. Ch 1, turn. Rep rows 1 and 2 of woven sc pat twice**. Change to smaller hook and sc.

Beg Chart 2
Work 8-st rep 20 times, then work first 7 sts once more. Cont as established through chart row 5. Change to larger hook and MC.
Next row (WS) Sc in first sc, *ch 1, skip next sc, sc in next sc; rep from * to end. Ch 1, turn. Rep rows 1 and 2 of woven sc pat once, end last row by joining A. Change to smaller hook.
Next row (RS) With A, sc in first sc, *draw up a long loop in next ch-1 sp 3 rows below, yo and through 2 lps—long sc made, skip next ch-1 sp (behind long sc), sc in next sc, sc in next ch-1 sp, sc in next sc; rep from * to last 2 sts, long sc in next ch-1 sp 3 rows below,

skip next ch-1 sp, sc in last sc. Ch 1, turn.
Next row Sc in back lp of first sc, *sc in front lp of next sc, sc in back lp of next sc; rep from * to end, join MC in last st. Ch 1, turn. Change to larger hook.
Next row (RS) Sc in first sc, *sc in next sc, ch 1, skip next sc; rep from * end sc in last 2 sts. Ch 1, turn. Rep row 2 of woven sc pat. Change to smaller hook and sc.

Beg Chart 3
Row 1 Work first 14 sts of chart, work 18-st rep 8 times, work last 9 sts of chart. Cont as established through chart row 19. Change to larger hook and MC.
Next row (WS) Sc in first sc, *ch 1, skip next sc, sc in next sc rep from * to end. Ch 1, turn. **Next row** Rep row 1 of woven sc pat, end by joining A. Ch 1, turn. Change to smaller hook.
Next row (WS) Sc in each st across. Ch 1, turn.
Next row Sc in back lp of first sc, *sc in front lp of next sc, sc in back lp of next sc; rep from * to end, join MC in last st. Ch 1, turn. Change to larger hook.
Next row (WS) Sc, in first sc, *ch 1, skip next sc, sc in next sc; rep from * to end. Ch 1, turn.
Next row Rep row 1 of woven sc pat, omitting turning ch at end of row. Fasten off.

(Continued on page 140)

Patchwork Panache

for intermediate knitters

Crochet any little touch of the blues with this patchwork afghan worked in a "Trip around the World" fashion. Start with a simple square as a building block, then crochet the bordering squares until the pattern is complete—no sewing is required. A lacy crocheted border adds the finishing touch. The "Patchwork Panache" afghan first appeared in the Fall '94 issue of *Family Circle Knitting*.

MATERIALS

- *Supersaver* Red Heart® by Coats and Clark, 8oz/227g balls, each approx 452yd/411m (acrylic)
  - 3 balls in #387 navy (A)
  - 2 balls in #382 blue (B)
  - I ball in #380 light blue (C)
- Size J/10 (6.00mm) crochet hook, OR SIZE TO OBTAIN GAUGE

FINISHED MEASUREMENTS

- 48 x 65"/122cm x 165cm

GAUGE

12 sts to 4"/10cm and 20 rows to 5"/ 9.5cm in single crochet using size J/10 (6.00mm) crochet hook.
Center motif and each rem square measures 3¾"/9.5cm across using size J/ 10 (6.00mm) crochet hook.
TAKE THE TIME TO CHECK YOUR GAUGE.

CENTER MOTIF (CM)

With hook and A, ch 4. Join with sl st to form ring. Ch 1.
Rnd 1 *Sc into ring, ch 2; rep from * 6 times, end sc into ring, hdc to beg sc. Ch 1.
Rnd 2 Work (sc, ch 2, sc) in ch-2 sp, *ch 1, sc in next ch-2 sp, ch 1, work (sc, ch 2, sc) in next ch-2 sp; rep from * twice, end ch 1, sc in next sp, st st to beg sc. Sl st along edge to ch-2 sp. Ch 1.
Rnd 3 Sc in same ch-2 sp, *ch 1, skip sc and ch-1 sp, work (2 dc, ch 2, 2 dc) in next sc, ch 1, sc in corner ch-2 sp; rep from * 3 times, end last rep ch 1, sl st to beg sc. Ch 1.
Rnd 4 Work 10 sc along each side as foil:

work I sc in each ch-1 sp and dc, 2 scs in each sc and work (sc, ch 2, sc) in each corner ch-2 sp. Join with sl st to beg ch. Fasten off.

First rnd (S1-S4)

S1 With RS of center motif facing and A, join yarn to any corner ch-2 sp. Ch 12.
Row 1 (RS) Sc in 2nd ch from hook, *ch 1, skip I ch, sc in next ch; rep from * 4 times-6 scs and 5 ch-1 sps. Sl st in first sc at side edge of center motif, then in 2nd sc. Ch 1, turn at end of this and all foll rows.
Row 2 (WS) Sc in first sc, *ch 1, skip next ch-1 sp, sc in next sc; rep from * across.
Row 3 Rep row 2, working sl st in 3rd, then 4th sc at side edge of center motif.
Rows 4-11 Rep row 2, working st st in 5th and 6th sc (row 5), 7th and 8th sc (row 7) and 9th and 10th sc (row 9). On row 11, sl st into ch-2 sp * Do not fasten off. S2 Ch 12. Rep rows I11 of St. In same way, work S3 and S4.

2nd rnd (S5-S12)

S5 With 13, join yarn to 11th foundation ch of St. Ch 12. Rep rows 1-11 of St. Do not fasten off. S6 Work square on top of square as

fell: *Ch 1, skip I sc, sc in next sc; rep from * 4 times-6 scs and 5 ch-1 sps. Sl st in first sc at side edge of adjoining motif (S2), then in 2nd sc. Ch 1, turn at end of this and all foll rows. Rep rows 2-11 of S 1. **S7** Ch 12. Work rows 1 -11 of St. **S8** Ch 1. Work square on top of square by rep S6, working across side of S2. **S9** Rep ST **S10** Ch 1. Rep S6, working across side of S3. **S11** Ch 12. Rep ST **S12** Ch 1. Rep S6, working across side of S4.

3rd-5th rnds

Work in same way as 2nd rnd, using C for 3rd rnd, B for 4th rnd and A for 5th rnd. Width established-I I squares wide.

Partial rnd 6

Join A to upper right corner of first square of 5th rnd, ch 1 and, working square on top of square as before, work around half of piece. In same way, join A and complete 2nd half.

Partial rnd 7

Join B to upper right corner of first square of last rnd. Complete as for partial rnd 6. Length established-15 squares long.

(Continued on page 141)

Weekend Sampler

for intermediate knitters

The building blocks of a great afghan starts with intriguing colors, interesting stitches, and a clever arrangement of textures. This cozy and charming sampler afghan, designed by Gloria Tracy, is joined together with contrasting yarn, creating a windowpane effect. The afghan was featured in the Spring/Summer '01 issue of *Family Circle Easy Knitting*.

MATERIALS
■ Creme Bruleé by K1C2, LLC, 1¾ oz/50g balls, each approx 131yd/120m (wool)
  7 balls in #210 brick (A)
  3 balls each in #849 rust (B) #299 orange (C), and #235 plum (E)
  2 balls in #294 peach (D)
■ Size H/8 (5mm) crochet hook OR SIZE TO OBTAIN GAUGE

FINISHED MEASUREMENTS
■ 32" x 47"/81cm x 119cm

GAUGE
1 square to 6"/15.5cm using size H/8 (5mm) crochet hook.
TAKE TIME TO CHECK YOUR GAUGE.

STITCHES USED

Mesh stitch (1)
Each square is 21 sts by 20 rows.

Double single crochet stitch (dsc)
Insert hook from front to back into 2nd ch from hook, yo and pull through, yo and draw through 1 lp yo and draw through 2 lps. Ch 23.
Row 1 Skip 2 ch (counts as dsc), dsc into next st, *skip 1 ch, 2 dsc into next ch; rep from * to last 2 ch, skip 1 ch, 2 dsc into last ch, turn.
Row 2 Ch 2, dsc into first st, *skip 1 st, 2 dsc into next st; rep from * to last 2 sts, skip 1 st, 2 dsc into last st, turn.
Rep row 2 for mesh st.

Block stitch (2)
Each square is 22 sts by 16 rows.
Ch 23.
Row 1 Sc in 2nd ch from hook, *ch 2, skip 2 ch, sc in next ch; rep from * to end, turn.

Row 2 Ch 4 (counts as dc and 1 ch), *3 dc in ch-2 sp, ch 1; rep from * to last st, dc in last st, turn.
Row 3 Ch 1, sc in first ch-1 sp, *ch 2, sc in next ch-1 sp; rep from * to end, turn.
Rep rows 2 and 3 for block st.

Shell ripple (3)
Each square is 22 sts by 13 rows.
Ch 25.
Row 1 Dc in 4th ch from hook, ch 1, dc in same ch as previous st, skip 2 ch, *2 dc in next ch, ch 1, 2 dc in same ch, skip 2 ch, dc in next ch, ch 1, dc in same ch, skip 2 ch; rep from * to last 3 ch, skip 2 ch, dc in last ch, turn.
Row 2 Ch 3, *2 dc in ch-1 sp, ch 1, 2 dc in same ch-1 sp, dc in next ch-1 sp, ch 1, dc in same ch-1 sp; rep from * to last ch-1 sp, 2 dc in ch-1 sp, ch 1, 2 dc in same ch-1 sp, dc in top of tch, turn.
Row 3 Ch 3, *dc in ch-1 sp, ch 1, dc in same ch-1 sp, 2 dc in next ch-1 sp, ch 1, 2 dc in same ch-1 sp; rep from * to last ch-1 sp, dc in ch-1 sp, ch 1, sc in same ch-1 sp, dc in top of tch, turn.
Rep rows 2 and 3 for shell ripple, working last rows as foll: Ch 1, sk next dc, *sc in each of next dc, ch-1 sp and next dc, skip next dc; rep from * to last st, sc in last st.

Ridge stitch (4)
Each square is 24 sts by 15 rows.
Ch 27.
Row 1 Insert hook in 2nd ch from hook and draw through lp, skip 1 ch, insert hook through next ch and draw through lp (3 lps on hook), [yo and draw through 2 lps] twice, *insert hook through horizontal crossbar of st just worked, yo and draw through lp, insert hook through next ch and draw through lp (3 lps on hook), [yo and draw through 2 lps] twice; rep from * to end, turn.
Row 2 Ch 3, work as for row 1, working into sts instead of chains.
Rep row 2 for ridge st.

Triple tucks (5)
Each square is 22 sts by 33 rows
Ch 23.
Row 1 Sc in 2nd ch from hook and in each ch to end, turn.
Row 2 (RS) Ch 1, sc in each sc, turn.
Row 3 Ch 4 (counts as 1 tr), tr in back lp of 2nd sc and in back lp of each sc to end, turn.
Row 4 Ch 1, *sc in back lp of each tr and in back lp of corresponding sc in row below; rep from *, end last st in top of tch, turn.
Row 5 Ch 1, sc in each sc, turn,
Rep rows 2-5 for triple tucks.

(Continued on page 142)

Afghan Basics

Made with love, an afghan makes the perfect gift for friends and family. Most are easy to make, some in squares and strips for effect or added portability, and can be finished relatively quickly. Since there is no shaping required, knitting and finishing are simple. This diverse selection will satisfy all tastes and skill levels, and spark the interest of novices and experts alike.

All the designs in this book can be altered in size to make them larger or smaller. To adjust the pattern, simply use the traditional method of increasing or decreasing the number of rows to achieve the desired size. Some of the afghans may be knit in the round from the center out. To adjust the finished size of these styles, work fewer or more rounds than specified. You can also change the yarn weight and/or needle size to create a new-sized afghan. Remember to adjust yarn requirements accordingly.

YARN SELECTION

For an exact reproduction of the blanket photographed, use the yarn listed in the materials section of the pattern. We've selected yarns that are readily available in the U.S. and Canada at the time of printing. The Resources list on page 143 provides addresses of yarn distributors. Contact them for the name of a retailer in your area.

YARN SUBSTITUTION

You may wish to substitute yarns. Perhaps you want an incredible yarn to coordinate with the family room, maybe a new afghan project is the perfect opportunity to incorporate leftovers from your yarn stash, or the yarn simply may not be available in your area. An afghan allows you to be creative, but you'll need to knit to the given gauge to obtain the knitted measurements with the substitute yarn (See "Gauge" on this page). Make pattern adjustments where necessary. Be sure to consider how different yarn types (chenille,

mohair, bouclé, etc.) will affect the final appearance of your afghan.

Some of the most common fibers used for afghans are acrylic yarns, which are lightweight and machine-washable; wools, which have incredible warmth; and cottons which are most suitable for warmer climates.

After you've successfully gauge-swatched a substitute yarn, you'll need to figure out how much of the substitute yarn the project requires.

HOW MUCH IS ENOUGH?

Step One

Determine the quantity of yarn needed to complete the project in the yarn listed in the pattern.

1. Find the number of balls requires for each color.

2. Find the number of yards (or meters) per ball or skein of that yarn. This information is included in the Materials section of all the patterns.

3. Multiply the number of yards (or meters) in each ball times the number of balls. Example: Let's say the pattern requires nine balls of yarn, and each ball is made up of 200 yards (182m). Multiple 9 times 200.

9 x 200 = 1,800 yards (or 9 x 182 = 1,638 meters)

1800 yards (or 1,638 meters) is the total yardage required. Write down this number, and keep it handy.

Step Two

Figure out the new quantity.

1. Determine the number of yards (or meters) per ball or skein of your new yarn. The yardage should be listed on the ball band or skein tag.

2. Divide the total yardage required (from Step One) by the yardage of your new yarn. Example: Let's say your new ball of yarn has a yardage of 109 yards (100 meters).

1,800/109 (or 1638/100)=16.5 balls.

Since you can't buy half of a ball, you need 17 balls of your replacement yarn.

If more than one yarn is used in the pattern, repeat steps 1 and 2.

Tip: Make sure that you are consistent when you use yards or meters. Stick with one system. If you multiplied yards times the number of balls, make sure you divide by yards, not meters, for the replacement ball.

FOLLOWING CHARTS

Charts provide a convenient way to follow colorwork, lace, cable and other stitch patterns at a glance. Family Circle Easy Afghans stitch charts utilize the universal knitting language of "symbolcraft." Unless otherwise indicated, read charts from right to left on right side (RS)

GAUGE

Most afghan patterns don't rely on perfect fit as a garment would, but it is still important to knit a gauge swatch. If the gauge is incorrect, a colorwork pattern may become distorted. The type of needles used—straight, circular, wood or metal—will influence gauge, so knit your swatch with the needles you plan to use for the project. Measure gauge as illustrated here. (Launder and block your gauge swatch before taking measurements). Try different needle sizes until your sample measures the required number of stitches and rows. To get fewer stitches to the inch/cm, use larger needles; to get more stitches to the inch/cm, use smaller needles. It's a good idea to keep your gauge swatch to test any embroidery or embellishment, as well as blocking, and cleaning methods.

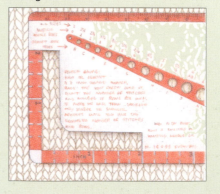

---

rows and from left to right on wrong side (WS) rows, repeating any stitch and row repeats as directed in the pattern. Posting a self-adhesive note under your working row is an easy way to keep track of your place on a chart.

COLORWORK KNITTING

Two main types of colorwork are explored in this book.

Intarsia

Intarsia is accomplished with separate bobbins of individual colors. This method is ideal for large blocks of color or for motifs that aren't repeated close together. When changing colors, always pick up the new color and wrap around the old color to prevent holes.

Stranding

When motifs are closely placed, colorwork is accomplished by stranding along two or more colors per row, creating "floats" on the wrong side of the fabric. When using this method, twist yarns on WS to prevent holes and strand loosely to keep knitting from puckering.

Note that yarn amounts have been calculated for the colorwork method suggested in the pattern. Knitting a stranded pattern with intarsia bobbins will take less yarn, while stranding an intarsia pattern will require more yarn.

BLOCKING

Blocking is the best way to shape pattern pieces and smooth knitted edges. However, some yarns, such as chenilles and ribbons, do not benefit from blocking. Choose a blocking method using information on the yarn care label and, when in doubt, test-block your gauge swatch.

Wet Block Method

Using rust-proof pins, pin the finished blanket to measurements on a flat surface and lightly dampen using a spray bottle. Allow to dry before removing the pins.

FINISHING

Since afghans are often knit in one piece, keep finishing in mind when beginning your project.
1. Because the back-side of the fabric will be seen when the afghan is used, you must be ready for the reverse to be on display. Think about using a stitch that is reversible, or one that looks good on both sides.
2. Consider adding border stitches to your blanket so that it has a built-in finish (many

border stitches will also help the blanket lie flat).
3. When adding a new yarn, be careful to do so at a place where you can easily weave the ends in, such as the sides, as there is frequently no "wrong side" on an afghan.

ASSEMBLY

There are several ways to construct an afghan in one piece, squares, strips, or sections. If the blanket is knit in one piece, try working back and forth on a long circular needle (29"- 60"/74cm –150cm). It will make it easier to accommodate the large number of stitches and keep you from poking the person next to you with your needle if you're working on a bus, train, or plane. An edging may be necessary to make the blanket lie flat—in some designs the border is knit in, in others it is picked up and knit or crocheted after the blanket is completed.

A pieced blanket is particularly suited to knitting on the run or sharing the work with others for a group gift. In this method, the pieces that make up the blanket are knit separately, then joined together to form the finished piece. Try using a contrasting color to join the pieces together and make this a feature of your design.

Joining can be done using these methods:
1. Sewing, using the traditional seaming method used for sweaters.
2. Crocheting, using either slip stitch or single crochet.
3. Embroidery, using a decorative stitch such as whip stitch or herringbone.

Steam Block Method

Pin the finished blanket to measurements with the wrong side of the knitting facing up. Steam lightly, holding the iron 2"/5cm above the work. Do not press the iron onto the knitting as it will flatten the stitches.

CARE

Refer to the yarn label for the recommended cleaning method. Many of the afghans in the book can be either washed by hand, or in the

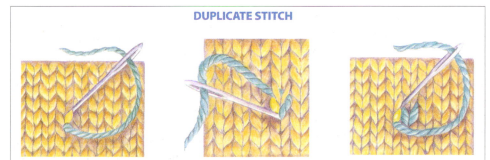

DUPLICATE STITCH

Duplicate stitch covers a knit stitch. Bring the needle up below the stitch to be worked. Insert the needle under both loops one row above and pull it through. Insert it back into the stitch below and through the center of the next stitch in one motion, as shown.

WORKING WITH RIBBON YARNS

- Place a nylon spool protector (a tube of netting) or a tube cut from an old stocking around your ball of ribbon so it won't unwind too fast. Slinky ribbon yarns slide off the ball very easily causing tangles or knots.
- Avoid pulling the ribbon. Keep a light hold as ribbons have a great deal of stretch and can distort when pulled.
- As with chenille, avoid over-twisting. A ribbon will have the best appearance when it lays flat.
- Clean your hands before knitting. Natural oils may stain or stiffen the rayon fiber used in most ribbons and some chenilles.
- Use non-slip needles. Needles of bamboo or wood will give you more control when working with slippery yarns.

water with a mild detergent. Do not agitate, and do not soak for more than 10 minutes. Rinse gently with tepid water, then fold in a towel and gently press the water out. Lay flat to dry away from excess heat and light. Check the yarn band for any specific care instructions such as dry cleaning or tumble drying.

TASSELS

Cut a piece of cardboard to the desired length of the tassel. Wrap yarn around the cardboard. Knot a piece of yarn tightly around one end, cut as shown, and remove the cardboard. Wrap and tie yarn around the tassel about 1"/2.5cm down from the top to secure the fringe.

FRINGE

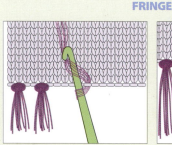

Simple fringe: Cut yarn twice desired length plus extra for knotting. On wrong side, insert hook from front to back through piece and over folded yarn. Pull yarn through. Draw ends through and tighten. Trim yarn.

Knotted fringe: After working a simple fringe (it should be longer to allow for extra knotting), take one half of the strands from each fringe and knot them with half the strands from the neighboring fringe.

POMPOMS

POMPOM TEMPLATE

1 Following the template, cut two circular pieces of cardboard.

2 Hold the circles together and wrap the yarn tightly around the cardboard several times. Secure and carefully cut the yarn.

3 Tie a piece a yarn tightly between the two circles. Remove the cardboard and trim the pompom to the desired size.

KNITTING NEEDLES		CROCHET HOOKS	
US	METRIC	US	METRIC
0	2 mm	14 steel	.60mm
1	2.25 mm	12 steel	.75mm
2	2.5 mm	10 steel	1.00mm
3	3 mm	6 steel	1.50mm
4	3.5 mm	5 steel	1.75mm
5	3.75 mm		
6	4 mm	B/1	2.00mm
7	4.5 mm	C/2	2.50mm
8	5 mm	D/3	3.00mm
9	5.5 mm	E/4	3.50mm
10	6 mm	F/5	4.00mm
10½	6.5, 7, 7.5mm	G/6	4.50mm
11	8 mm	H/8	5.00mm
13	9 mm	I/9	5.50mm
15	10 mm	J/10	6.00mm
17	12.75 mm		
19	16 mm		6.50mm
35	19 mm	K/10½	7.00mm

BASIC STITCHES

GARTER STITCH
Knit every row. Circular knitting: knit one round, then purl one round.

STOCKINETTE STITCH
Knit right-side rows and purl wrong-side rows. Circular knitting: knit all rounds. (UK: stocking stitch)

REVERSE STOCKINETTE STITCH
Purl right-side rows and knit wrong-side rows. Circular knitting: purl all rounds. (UK: reverse stocking stitch)

Knit/Crochet Terms and Abbreviations

approx approximately

beg begin(ning)

bind off Used to finish an edge and keep stitches from unraveling. Lift the first stitch over the second, the second over the third, etc. (UK: cast off)

cast on A foundation row of stitches placed on the needle in order to begin knitting.

CC contrast color

ch chain(s)

cm centimeter(s)

cont continu(e)(ing)

dc double crochet (UK: tr–treble)

dec decrease(ing)–Reduce the stitches in a row (knit 2 together).

dpn double-pointed needle(s)

dtr double treble (UK: trtr—triple treble)

foll follow(s)(ing)

g gram(s)

garter stitch Knit every row. Circular knitting: knit one round, then purl one round.

grp(s) group(s)

hdc half double crochet (UK: htr–half treble)

inc increase(ing)–Add stitches in a row (knit into the front and back of a stitch).

k knit

k2tog knit 2 stitches together

LH left-hand

lp(s) loop(s)

m meter(s)

M1 make one stitch–With the needle tip, lift the strand between last stitch worked and next stitch on the left-hand needle and knit into the back of it. One stitch has been added.

MC main color

mm millimeter(s)

no stitch On some charts, "no stitch" is indicated with shaded spaces where stitches have been decreased or not yet made. In such cases, work the stitches of the chart, skipping over the "no stitch" spaces.

oz ounce(s)

p purl

p2tog purl 2 stitches together

pat(s) pattern

pick up and knit (purl) Knit (or purl) into the loops along an edge.

pm place markers–Place or attach a loop of contrast yarn or purchased stitch marker as indicated.

psso pass slip stitch(es) over

rem remain(s)(ing)

rep repeat

rev St st reverse stockinette stitch–Purl right-side rows, knit wrong-side rows. Circular knitting: purl all rounds. (UK: reverse stocking stitch)

rnd(s) round(s)

RH right-hand

RS right side(s)

sc single crochet (UK: dc–double crochet)

sk skip

SKP Slip 1, knit 1, pass slip stitch over knit 1.

SK2P Slip 1, knit 2 together, pass slip stitch over the knit 2 together.

sl slip–An unworked stitch made by passing a stitch from the left-hand to the right-hand needle as if to purl.

sl st slip stitch (UK: sc–single crochet)

sp(s) space(s)

ssk slip, slip, knit–Slip next 2 stitches knitwise, one at a time, to right-hand needle. Insert tip of left-hand needle into fronts of these stitches from left to right. Knit them together. One stitch has been decreased.

sssk Slip next 3 sts knitwise, one at a time, to right-hand needle. Insert tip of left-hand needle into fronts of these stitches from left to right. Knit them together. Two stitches have been decreased.

st(s) stitch(es)

St st Stockinette stitch–Knit right-side rows, purl wrong-side rows. Circular knitting: knit all rounds. (UK: stocking stitch)

tbl through back of loop

t-ch turning chain

tog together

tr treble (UK: dtr—double treble)

trtr triple treble (UK: qtr—quadruple treble)

WS wrong side(s)

wyib with yarn in back

wyif with yarn in front

work even Continue in pattern without increasing or decreasing. (UK: work straight)

yd yard(s)

yo yarn over–Make a new stitch by wrapping the yarn over the right-hand needle. (UK: yfwd, yon, yrn)

* = Repeat directions following * as many times as indicated.

[ ] = Repeat directions inside brackets as many times as indicated.

(continued from page 38)

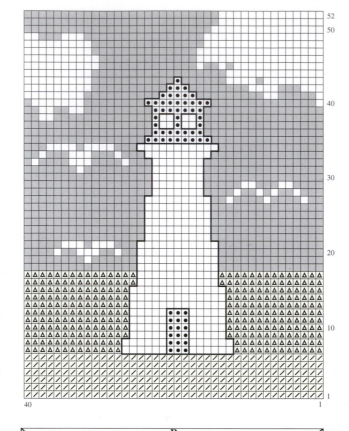

Color key

- ⊙ Red (A)
- ▢ Lt. Blue (D)
- ▲ Royal (E)
- ◪ Med. Green (F)
- ▢ White (G)

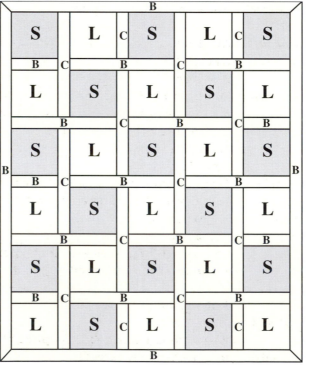

L = Lighthouse square

S = Seed stitch square

C = Grid panel in Navy (C)

B = Grid panel & border
in Dk. Green (B)

Row 2 and all WS rows Purl.
Row 3 1 selvage st, *k1, yo, SKP, k3, k2tog, yo, k2; rep from * to end.
Row 5 1 selvage st, *k2, yo, SKP, k1, k2tog, yo, k3; rep from * to end.
Row 7 1 selvage st, *k3, yo, SK2P, yo, k4; rep from * to end.
Row 9 1 selvage st, *k2, k2tog, yo, k1, yo, SKP, k3; rep from * to end.
Row 11 1 selvage st, *k1, k2tog, yo, k3, yo, SKP, k2; rep from * to end.
Row 13 1 selvage st, *k2tog, yo, k5, yo, SKP, k1; rep from * to end.
Row 15 K2tog, *yo, k7, yo, SK2P; rep from *, end SKP.
Row 16 Purl.
Rep rows 1-16 for square 5 until piece measures 10"/25.5cm. Bind off.

PATTERN 6
Cast on 43 sts.
Row 1 1 selvage st, *p3, k1 tbl, p1, k1 tbl, p1, k1 tbl, p2; rep from *, end p1, 1 selvage st.
Row 2 K the knit sts and p the purl sts.
Rep rows 1 and 2 for square 6 until piece measures 10"/25.5cm. Bind off.

PATTERN 7
Cast on 42 sts.
Row 1 1 selvage st, *k2, p2; rep from *, end 1 selvage st.
Rows 2 and 4 K the knit sts and p the purl sts.

Row 3 1 selvage st, *p2, k2; rep from * to end.
Rep rows 1-4 for square 7 until piece measures 10"/25.5cm. Bind off.

PATTERNS 8
Cast on 42 sts.
Row 1 1 selvage st, *k3, p1; rep from *, end 1 selvage st.
Row 2 1 selvage st, *k2, p1, k1; rep from *, end 1 selvage st.
Rep rows 1 and 2 for square 8 until piece measures 10"/25.5cm. Bind off.

PATTERN 9
Cast on 44 sts.
Row 1 Knit.
Row 2 and all WS rows Purl.
Row 3 1 selvage st, k3, *sl 3 sts to cn and hold to front, k3, k3 from cn, k6; rep from *, end k3, 1 selvage st.
Row 5 Knit.
Row 7 1 selvage st, k3, *k6, sl 3 sts to cn and hold to back, k3, k3 from cn; rep from *, end k3, 1 selvage st.
Row 8 Purl.
Rep rows 3-8 for square 9 until piece measures 10"/25.5cm. Bind off.

PATTERN 10
Cast on 38 sts.
Row 1 1 selvage st, *p2, k2, p2, k1, p2, k2, p1; rep from *, end 1 selvage st.

Row 2 and all WS rows K the knit sts and p the purl sts.
Row 3 1 selvage st, *p1, k2, p2, k3, p2, k2; rep from *, end 1 selvage st.
Row 5 1 selvage st, *k2, p2, k2, p1, k2, p2, k1; rep from *, end 1 selvage st.
Row 7 1 selvage st, *k1, p2, k2, p3, k2, p2; rep from *, end 1 selvage st.
Row 8 Rep row 2.
Rep rows 1-8 for square 10 until piece measures 10"/25.5cm. Bind off.

FINISHING
Block to measurements. Sew blocks tog as desired with 5 squares wide by 6 squares long.

BORDER (OPTIONAL)
Cut two pieces of fabric each 7" x 61"/17.5cm x 155cm. Make a ½"/1.5cm seam allowance at each short end of fabric. With WS of afghan facing, and working along one longer end, lay RS of fabric along edge of afghan, ½"/1.5cm in from edge and sew in place. Fold fabric in half to RS, and making a ½"/1.5cm seam allowance, sew in place. Work in same way along other long end.
Cut two pieces each 7" x 47"/17.5cm x 119.5cm. Make seam allowances and sew to short ends of afghan in same way.

Stitch Key

☐ K on RS, p on WS

⊟ P on RS, k on WS

◿◺ [k3tog, p3tog, k3tog] in next 3 sts

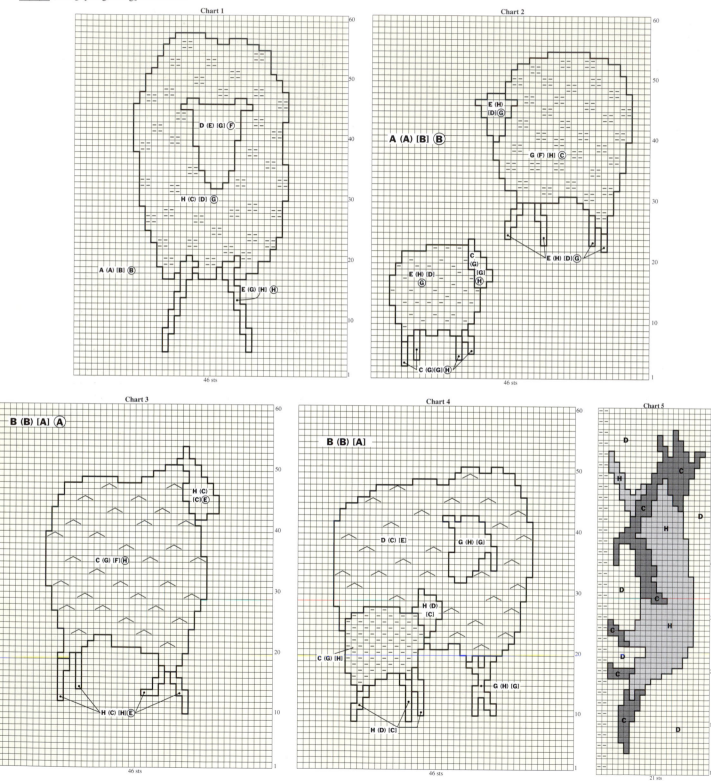

Square 1

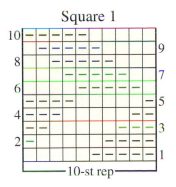

└─10-st rep─┘

Square 2

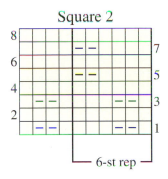

└─ 6-st rep ─┘

Square 3

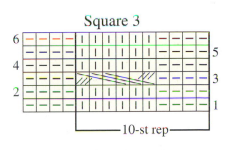

└─10-st rep─┘

Square 4

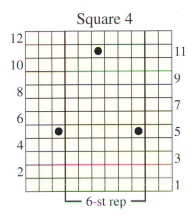

└─ 6-st rep ─┘

Square 5

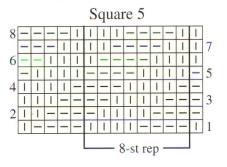

└─ 8-st rep ─┘

Square 6

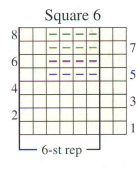

└─ 6-st rep ─┘

Afghan Square Diagram

5	3	1	6	4	2
4	6	5	2	1	3
1	2	3	4	5	6
2	4	6	1	3	5
3	1	2	5	6	4
4	6	5	2	1	3
5	3	1	6	4	2
6	5	4	3	2	1

Stitch Key

□ or ① k on RS, p on WS

— p on RS, k on WS

● Bobble

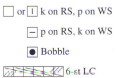 6-st LC

Cream of the Crop

(continued from page 66)

Chart 2

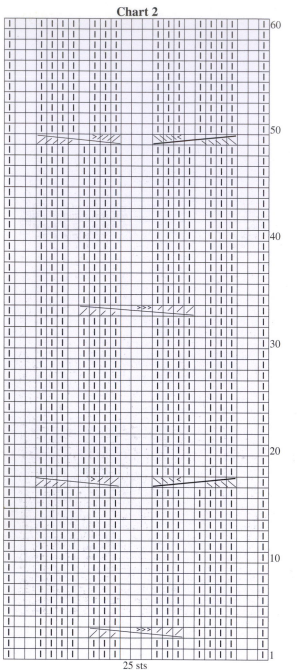

25 sts

Chart 1

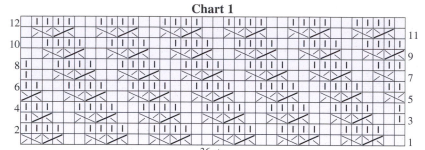

36 sts

Stitch Key

| | K on RS, p on WS |
| P on RS, k on WS |
| RT |
| LT |
| 4/4 RPC |
| 4/4 LPC |
| 5/3 RPC |
| 5/3 LPC |
| 9-st LPC |
| 11-st LPC |

Chart 3

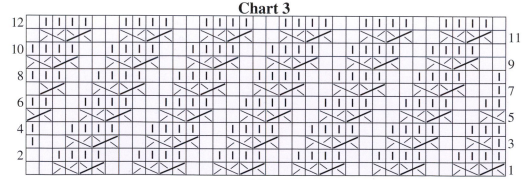

36 sts

Chart 1

Square 1   Square 2

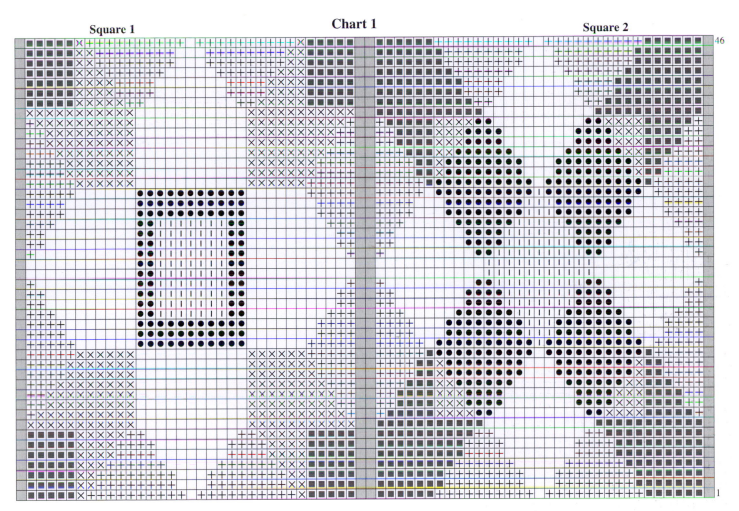

Color Key

Plum (A)

Wine (B)

Dk gold (C)

Olive (D)

Lt. green (E)

Dk pink (F)

Garter st with plum (A)

**Heart Afghan
Placement Chart**

#9	#10	#11	#12	#11	#10	#9
#5	#6	#7	#8	#7	#6	#5
#1	#2	#3	#4	#3	#2	#1

rep 3 times

work 1 time

Symbol	Stitch
/	Straight st
–	Running st
∪∩∪	Chain st
●	French knot

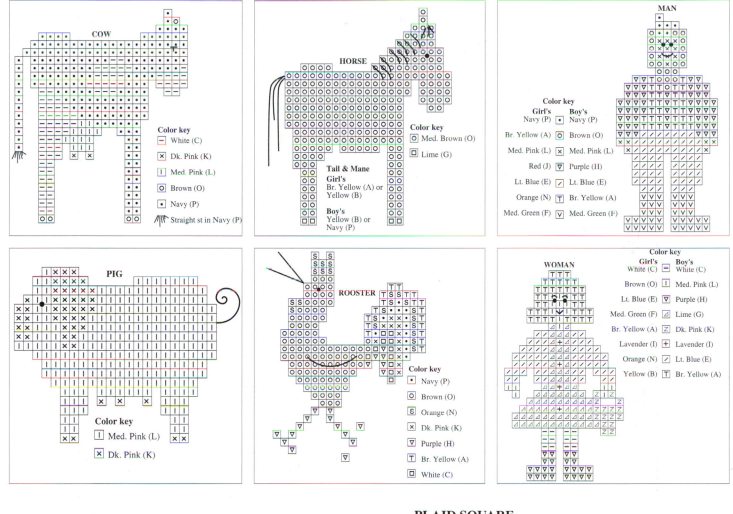

COW

Color key
- — White (C)
- ✕ Dk. Pink (K)
- | Med. Pink (L)
- ⊙ Brown (O)
- • Navy (P)
- ⫽ Straight st in Navy (P)

HORSE

Color key
- ⊙ Med. Brown (O)
- ☐ Lime (G)

Tail & Mane
Girl's
Br. Yellow (A) or
Yellow (B)
Boy's
Yellow (B) or
Navy (P)

MAN

Color key
Girl's	Boy's
Navy (P) •	Navy (P)
Br. Yellow (A) ⊙	Brown (O)
Med. Pink (L) ✕	Med. Pink (L)
Red (J) ▽	Purple (H)
Lt. Blue (E) ⫽	Lt. Blue (E)
Orange (N) T	Br. Yellow (A)
Med. Green (F) ∨	Med. Green (F)

PIG

Color key
- | Med. Pink (L)
- ✕ Dk. Pink (K)

ROOSTER

Color key
- • Navy (P)
- ⊙ Brown (O)
- S Orange (N)
- ✕ Dk. Pink (K)
- ▽ Purple (H)
- T Br. Yellow (A)
- ☐ White (C)

WOMAN

Color key
Girl's	Boy's
White (C) —	White (C)
Brown (O)	Med. Pink (L)
Lt. Blue (E) ▽	Purple (H)
Med. Green (F) ∠	Lime (G)
Br. Yellow (A) Z	Dk. Pink (K)
Lavender (I) +	Lavender (I)
Orange (N) ∕	Lt. Blue (E)
Yellow (B) T	Br. Yellow (A)

Stitch & Color key
- | Dk. color, k on RS, p on WS
- — Dk. color, k on RS, p on WS
- ✕ Lt. color, k on RS, p on WS
- ⊙ White, k on RS, p on WS

- — Dk. color, p on RS, k on WS
- ✕ Lt. color, p on RS, k on WS
- ⊙ White, p on RS, k on WS

PLAID SQUARE

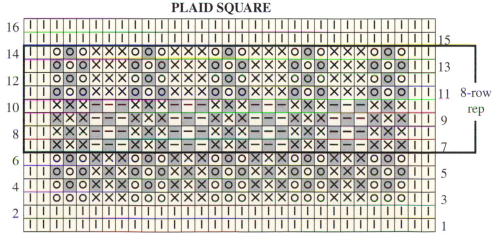

8-row rep

Next row From RS, with smaller hook, join MC with sl st in first sc. Ch 1, sc in same st, joining A in last 2 lps;*with A, long sc in next ch-1 sp 2 rows below, joining MC in last 2 lps, skip next ch-1 sp (behind long sc); with MC, sc in next ch-1 sp, joining A in last 2 lps; rep from * to last 2 sts, with A, long sc in next ch-1 sp 2 rows below, joining MC in last 2 lps; with MC, sc in last sc. Ch 1, turn. Change to smaller hook and sc.

Beg Chart 4

Work 5 rows chart 4 same as chart 2. Fasten off. Change to larger hook and MC.

Next row (WS) Sc in first sc, *ch 1, skip next sc, sc in next sc; rep from * to end. Ch 1, turn. Rep rows 1 and 2 of woven sc pat twice***. Rep from ** to *** twice more, then from ** to ** once. Fasten off.

FINISHING

Edging

From RS, with smaller hook, join A with sl st in one corner of throw. Ch 1, 3 sc in same sp. Work 1 rnd sc evenly around outer edge of throw, working 3 sc in each corner. Join with sl st in first sc. Ch 1, do not turn. Working backwards sc (from left to right), sc in each sc around, join last sc with sl st in first sc. Fasten off.

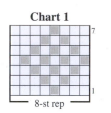

Chart 1

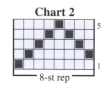

Chart 2

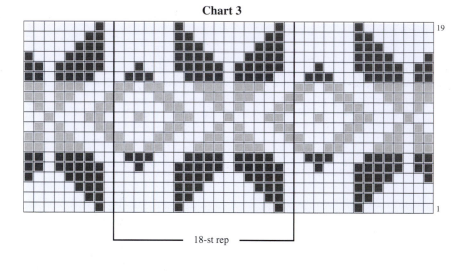

Chart 3

Color Key

☐ Beige (MC)

▨ Lt brown A

■ Dk brown C

Chart 4

(continued from page 124)

Work across sides

Partial rnd 8 With C, work 5 squares across each side edge. Partial rnd 9 With B, work 4 squares across each side edge ' Partial rnd 10 With A, work 3 squares across each side edge. Partial rnd 11 With A, work 2 squares across each side edge.

CORNER SQUARES

With B, work final 4 corner squares.

BORDER

With RS facing, join A to corner and work 169 sc along length of piece. Ch 1, turn.

Row 1 Sc in first sc, *skip 2 sc, work (2 dc, ch 2, 2 de) in next sc (shell made), skip 2 sc, sc in next sc; rep from *. Ch 1, turn.

Row 2 Sc in first sc, *ch 2, (sc, ch 2, sc) in ch-2 sp, ch 2, (sc, ch 2, sc) in sc; rep from *, end last rep ch 2, sc in beg ch. Ch 3, turn.

Row 3 Dc in first sc, *skip ch-2 sp and sc, sc in ch-2 sp, skip sc and ch-2 sp, shell in next ch-2 sp; rep from *, end last rep skip sc and ch-2 sp, 2 dc in beg sc. Ch 1, turn.

Row 4 Sc in first dc, *ch 2, (sc, ch 2, sc) in next sc, ch 2, (sc-ch 2, sc) in ch-2 sp; rep from *, end last rep ch 2, sc to top of beg ch. Ch 1, turn.

Row 5 Sc in first sc, *skip ch-2 sp and sc, work shell in next ch-2 sp, skip sc and ch-2 sp, sc in next ch-2 sp; rep from *, end last rep skip sc and ch-2 sp, sc in beg sc. Ch 1, turn.

Row 6 Rep row 2. Ch 1, turn.

Row 7 Sc in first sc, *ch 2, (sc, ch 2, sc) in ch-2 sp of (sc, ch-2, sc) of previous row; rep from *, end ch 2, sc in beg sc. Fasten off. In same way, work border along opposite side. With RS facing, join A to corner of lengthwise border and work I I sc across border, 123 sc along width of piece, 11 sc along rem border145 sc. Work rows 1-7 of border as before. In same way, work border along rem side. Fasten off.

		S7		
	S8	S2	S6	
S9	S3	CM	S1	S5
	S10	S4	S12	
		S11		

Twisted loops (6)

Each square is 20 sts (19 lps) by 23 rows.
Ch 23.

Row 1 Sk 3 ch (counts as dc), dc in each ch to end, turn.

Row 2 *Ch 7, beg in 2nd st, sl st in back lp only, inserting hook from back to front; rep from *, end ch 7, sl st in top of tch, turn.

Row 3 Ch 3, beg in 2nd st, inserting hook from front to back, dc in each st through back lp only, turn.

Rep rows 2 and 3 for twisted loops.

Squares

In mesh st (1), make 6 with A and 4 with B.

In block st (2), make 4 with B and 4 with C.

In shell ripple (3), make 2 with, 2 with C and 1 with D.

In ridge st (4), make 4 with D.

In triple tucks (5), make 2 with A and 2 with C.

In twisted loops (6), make 4 with A.

FINISHING SQUARES

As each square is complete, using same color, work 21 sc along top edge to last st, work 3 sc in next st; work in same way for other three sides, sl st to first st.

With RS facing, leaving a 15"/38cm tail, join E with sc to lower left center corner st, ch 1, sc in same st, *ch 1, skip next st; rep from * along edge to corner, working sc, ch 1, sc into center corner st. Cont as established along each side, end with a ch 1 and sl st into first sc, Fasten off, leaving a 15"/38cm tail.

Joining squares

Hint Squares are connected with a rickrack st worked through the ch-1 spaces. To line up the spaces, run a small knitting needle in and out through the openings. Lay out the blocks foll the placement diagram. Work across each horizontal row, connecting the sides of adjoining squares using the rickrack edging as foll: With WS of squares tog, leaving a 15"/38cm tail, join at corner ch-1 sp with sc, sc into same sp, skip next st, *ch 1, (sl st, sc, sl st) into next ch-1 sp, skip next st; rep from * along edge to corner, ending ch 1, sl st, sc in corner ch-1 sp.

With E, join the horizontal rows tog as before and also working through the ch-1 spaces of each join. Work around outside edges as before.

Chained knots

If necessary, add 15"/38cm length of E in order to have four 15"/38cm strand on the RS at each junction. With two of the four strands crochet a ch, fasten off, leaving a 3"/7.5cm tail. Rep for other 2 strands. Coil chains in a circle, fasten down with 3"/7.5cm tails. Rep for all junctions.

A1	B2	A1	B2	A1
C2	A6	C3	A6	C2
B1	D4	A5	D4	B1
A3	C5	D3	C5	A3
B1	D4	A5	D4	B1
C2	A6	C3	A6	C2
A1	B2	A1	B2	A1

Resources

Berroco, Inc.
14 Elmdale Road
PO Box 367
Uxbridge, MA 01569

Bernat®
PO Box 40
Listowel, ON N4W 3H3
Canada

Brown Sheep Co.
100662 County Road 16
Mitchell, NE 69357

Caron International
P O Box 222
Washington, NC 27889

Cascade Yarns
2401 Utah Ave. S
Suite 505
Seattle, WA 98134

Classic Elite Yarns
300A Jackson Ave.
Lowell, MA 01854
www.classiceliteyarns.com

Cleckheaton
distributed by
Plymouth Yarns

Coats & Clark, Inc.
Attn: Consumer Service
PO Box 12229
Greenville, SC 299612-02229

Crystal Palace Yarns
3006 San Pablo Ave.
Berkeley, CA 94702

JCA
35 Scales Lane
Townsend, MA 01469

K1C2, LLC
2220 Eastman Ave. #105
Ventura, CA 93003

Lane Borgosesia
PO Box 217
Colorado Springs, CO 80903

Lily®
PO Box 40
Listowel, ON N4W 3H3
Canada

Lion Brand Yarns Co.
34 West 15th Street
New York, NY 10011
www.lionbrand.com

Mission Falls
distributed by
Unique Kolours

Naturally
distributed by
S. R Kertzer, Ltd.

Patons®
PO Box 40
Listowel, ON N4W 3H3
Canada
www.patonsyarns.com

Plymouth Yarn
PO Box 28
Bristol, PA 19007

Reynolds
distributed by
JCA

Sesia
distributed by
Lane Borgosesia

S. R. Kertzer, Ltd.
105A Winges Road
Woodbridge, ON L4L 6C2
Canada
Tel: (800) 263-2354
www.kertzer.com

Unique Kolours
1428 Oak Lane
Downingtown, PA 19335

Unger
distributed by
JCA

We have made every effort to ensure the accuracy of the contents of this publication.
We are not responsible for any human or typographical errors.

Acknowledgements

There are many people who contributed to the making of this book, and most important, we would like to thank the previous editors of *Family Circle Easy Knitting* magazine, including Polly Roberts, Marilyn F. Cooperman, Lola Ehrlich, Margaret C. Korn, Meredith Gray Harris, Sonja Bjorklund Dagress, Nancy J. Thomas, Margery Winter, and Gay Bryant. We would also like to extend our appreciation and gratitude to all of the dedicated and knowledgeable *Family Circle Easy Knitting* staff members, past and present, for their skill, and countless hours of hard work in bringing the best of knitting to their readers. Special thanks also goes to the tireless knitters and contributing technical experts, without whom the magazine would not be possible.

Photo Credits

Paul Amato
(pp. 8, 12, 34, 44, 60, 70, 104, 110, 114, 118, 120, 122)

Robert Bonicoro
(pp. 42, 106)

Terrance Carney
(p. 90)

Andy Cohen
(pp. 10, 76, 78, 124)

Jack Deutsch
(p. 48)

Brian Kraus
(pp. 14, 16, 18, 22, 24, 26, 28, 36, 38, 50, 56, 58, 64, 66, 74, 80, 82, 86, 94, 96, 98, 100, 102)

Brian Kraus and Juan Rios
(pp. 62, 112)

Rudy Molacek
(p. 30)

Chris Pinto
(p. 46, 68)

VNU Syndications
(pp. 40, 84)